UNGRATEFUL

Jacques Chambers

Table of Contents

Chapter 1

The city of Portland, Oregon, basked in its usual rhythm of normalcy as the dawn broke over its skyline. The morning sun rose cautiously, casting pale yellow streaks across a sky painted with wisps of clouds. It was late spring, and the weather, caught in a delicate balance, neither swayed towards biting cold nor oppressive heat. Instead, it offered a crisp, gentle breeze that carried with it the faint aroma of rain-soaked earth and blooming flowers. The kind of morning that whispered promises of an uneventful yet comforting day.

Nestled within the urban sprawl was an apartment building that stood modestly against the backdrop of towering skyscrapers and dense foliage. It was neither new nor old, its beige façade weathered but sturdy, adorned with wooden shutters painted in a subdued forest green. The building exuded a charm that came from years of housing lives that ebbed and flowed like the tides—each apartment a silent witness to countless stories of love, loss, and everyday existence.

On the fourth floor of this building, one particular apartment came alive with the soft rustle of curtains drawn back from the windows. Inside, the living space was a cozy blend of modern convenience and personal touches. The walls, painted in a muted sage green, were adorned with framed photographs and abstract artwork. A plush gray sofa, slightly worn but inviting, took center stage in the living room, flanked by a glass coffee table bearing a stack of well-thumbed books and an assortment of coffee mugs.

The kitchen, separated by a sleek counter, bore the telltale signs of a hurried breakfast. A plate with toast crumbs sat abandoned beside a half-filled cup of coffee, still steaming faintly. The refrigerator door was cluttered with colorful magnets holding up grocery lists, children's drawings, and a Polaroid or two, hinting at the life lived within these walls.

The window in the living room framed a picture-perfect view of the bustling city below. From this vantage point, one could see the winding streets stretching out like veins, busy with early commuters. Cars honked in short bursts, blending into the background symphony of distant chatter and the occasional bark of a dog. Across the street, a row of cherry blossom trees stood in full bloom, their pink petals fluttering down like confetti, adding a touch of whimsy to the otherwise pragmatic cityscape.

Beyond the immediate urban scene, the hills of Portland rose in gentle slopes, dotted with evergreens that seemed to stretch endlessly toward the horizon. A light mist clung to their peaks, lending an ethereal quality to the view. On the farthest edge, the faint silhouette of Mount Hood stood as a silent sentinel, its snow-capped peak glistening under the soft light of the morning sun.

This apartment, this city, and this morning—all seemed to hum with an unspoken stillness, a calm that could only exist in the moments before life's unexpected twists made their presence known. Yet, for now, it was enough. Enough to breathe, to exist, and to soak in the beauty of the ordinary.

Inside the cozy apartment on the fourth floor, the serene atmosphere was disrupted by the unmistakable energy of Jasmine, a woman who never failed to make her presence known. In her late 20s, Jasmine embodied a bold and unapologetic confidence, her style as dazzling as her personality. Sprawled across the worn but inviting gray sofa, she scrolled through her phone with the finesse of someone entirely at ease with her domain.

Her nails—long, perfectly manicured, and painted a glittering gold—danced across the screen. The light from her phone cast a soft glow over her flawless mocha skin, highlighting her sharp cheekbones and the faint shimmer of her glossy lips. Jasmine's outfit, a hot pink tracksuit that clung to her form with just the right amount of sass, was paired with oversized hoop earrings and a stack of golden bangles that jingled softly as she moved. She radiated a sense of charisma that seemed to fill every corner of the room.

The coffee table in front of her bore the hallmarks of her morning ritual: a glossy fashion magazine flipped open to an article about celebrity trends, a nearly empty bag of spicy chips, and a lipstick tube lying on its side. Her phone dinged with notifications, but she barely glanced at them, her focus locked on the curated lives of influencers and celebrities.

The muted sage green walls of the apartment seemed almost too subdued in contrast to her vibrant energy. The framed photographs and abstract artwork lining the walls bore silent witness to her animated mutterings. "Girl, who told you to wear that?" she scoffed, swiping past an influencer's outfit that she deemed unworthy of her admiration.

The window, still open to the view of Portland's bustling streets, framed a city alive with movement. Jasmine occasionally glanced out, her hoop earrings catching the sunlight as she tilted her head. Her eyes lingered on the cherry blossoms fluttering in the breeze, their delicate beauty a quiet counterpoint to her bold demeanor.

A commercial blared from the TV, breaking her reverie. Jasmine groaned and reached for the remote, muting it without looking up from her phone. She shifted her position, one leg curling beneath her while the other dangled off the couch, her gold sneakers barely brushing the soft rug below.

"Ugh, where's my coffee?" she muttered to herself, her tone carrying equal parts annoyance and drama. The abandoned mug on the kitchen counter caught her eye, and she sighed. "I swear, I need an assistant."

Despite her larger-than-life persona, there was an authenticity to Jasmine that drew people in. Her confidence wasn't an act—it was a shield and a declaration, a reminder that she owned her space and her life unapologetically. As the cherry blossoms drifted down outside and the city hummed along with its usual rhythm, Jasmine's world was an unrelenting whirlwind of style, sass, and ambition.

The front door creaked open, its sound mingling with the distant hum of the bustling city outside. A middle-aged woman stepped in, her presence radiating warmth and calm. She carried a small leather-bound Bible in one hand and a neatly folded church bulletin in the other. Dressed in a simple yet elegant navy-blue dress with a lace collar, her face glowed with a quiet peace.

"Good morning," she greeted softly, her eyes falling on the young woman sprawled on the couch.

Jasmine, dressed in a hot pink tracksuit, barely looked up from her phone. Her fingers moved rapidly, scrolling and tapping as though the world existed only within the bright screen in her hand. "Morning, Mom. I can see that."

The woman sighed gently but smiled as she moved further into the room. She sat down beside Jasmine, placing her Bible and bulletin carefully on the coffee table. "Pastor Richards was asking about you today," she said, her voice tinged with gentle curiosity.

Jasmine paused briefly, her eyebrows lifting in faint amusement. "Oh, really? I'm flattered. Tell him I'm thriving."

Her mother tilted her head, her lips curving into a patient smile. "He said he hasn't seen you in a while. Wanted to know how you've been."

Finally setting her phone down, Jasmine leaned back into the couch cushions, her tone casual but with a hint of playfulness. "Mom, you know church isn't really my thing. It's great that it works for you, but let's not pretend I'm cut out to be the choir girl."

A soft chuckle escaped her mother as she adjusted the fabric of her dress. "I'm not asking you to join the choir, Jasmine. Just come, sit, listen. Sometimes it's not about being the 'type.' It's about finding peace."

Jasmine gave a dramatic sigh, crossing her arms over her chest. "I've got my own version of peace, Mom. Trust me."

Her mother's gaze softened as she studied Jasmine's face, a mix of amusement and concern flickering in her eyes. "I do trust you. Always. But life has a way of surprising us. Sometimes, it's nice to have something steady to hold on to."

Tilting her head, Jasmine let a small smirk creep onto her face. "If life throws me a curveball, I'll knock it out of the park. No offense to Pastor Richards, but I don't think he's got tips for that."

Her mother laughed, the sound warm and reassuring, her eyes crinkling at the corners. "Fair enough. But don't say I didn't warn you when you find yourself praying for a little guidance someday."

The playful exchange hung in the air, wrapping the room in a familiar comfort.

The conversation shifted when her mother picked up the church bulletin and glanced at it thoughtfully. "We're organizing a charity bake sale next weekend," she said. "The proceeds are going to the shelter downtown—the one near Pioneer Square."

Jasmine furrowed her brows slightly as she reached for a spicy chip from the bag on the coffee table. "The one that helps families get back on their feet?"

Her mother nodded. "That's the one. I was thinking you could help out. Maybe bake some of those cookies you're always so proud of."

Jasmine raised an eyebrow, popping the chip into her mouth. "You mean my perfect double-chocolate chunk cookies? The ones everyone loves?"

A grin spread across her mother's face. "Exactly those."

Jasmine pretended to deliberate, her lips pursed in exaggerated thought. "Hmm, I don't know. My cookies are a hot commodity. It could be dangerous putting them out there for free."

Her mother chuckled, patting Jasmine's hand gently. "Dangerous or not, I think it'd be nice. And besides, it might do you some good to get involved with the community."

Jasmine leaned forward, narrowing her eyes in mock suspicion. "Okay, I'll think about it. But only if you promise to keep Pastor Richards off my case. Deal?"

"Deal," her mother replied with a knowing smile.

As the morning stretched on, the apartment brimmed with the dynamic energy of their conversation. Jasmine, with her vibrant personality, filled the space with color, while her mother's steady calm provided a grounding force. The city outside carried on, cherry blossoms drifting down like confetti in the breeze.

Jasmine barely reacted, her attention glued to her phone, where an image of a glamorous celebrity showcasing a new luxury handbag dominated the screen. Her thumb hovered over the "like" button for a moment before she spoke, her tone distant. "I'm fine. He doesn't need to worry."

Her mother's face reflected a quiet mixture of concern and sadness. She leaned forward slightly, hoping to bridge the widening gap with warmth and conversation. "We had a lovely service today," she began, her voice carrying the enthusiasm of someone eager to share a meaningful experience.

"The choir sang one of your favorite hymns—'Amazing Grace.'" Her eyes softened with nostalgia. "And Sister Grace brought some homemade pies for everyone after the service. Oh, and we talked about organizing a charity drive for the less fortunate in our community. It was really inspiring."

Jasmine smirked faintly, her expression betraying her lack of interest. She finally glanced at her mother but only for a fleeting second before returning to the glow of her phone. "That's nice, Mom," she replied, her voice detached, as though the words were merely obligatory.

Her mother sighed softly, her gaze lingering on Jasmine, who continued scrolling through a curated world of perfection. Her fingers paused briefly on another post—a celebrity standing next to a gleaming luxury car, the caption boasting of success and extravagance.

The contrast between them was unmistakable. Jasmine, engrossed in a life of virtual glamour and material longing, and her mother, grounded in the simple joys of community, faith, and giving. It was a divide not of love but of values, one that neither fully understood nor could easily bridge.

Her mother reached out gently, placing her hand on Jasmine's arm. "You know," she said quietly, "it's okay to want nice things. But sometimes, the things we do for others bring a kind of joy you can't find anywhere else."

Jasmine looked up, her brow furrowed slightly, as if debating whether to respond. "Mom, I know you mean well, but not everyone gets the same kind of joy out of… church stuff or charity drives."

Her mother nodded thoughtfully, a patient smile gracing her lips. "Maybe not," she agreed, "but it doesn't hurt to try. Sometimes, giving back doesn't just help others—it helps you see the world differently. Helps you see yourself differently."

Jasmine shrugged, her gaze returning to the polished veneer of her digital escape. "Maybe," she said absently, though the words carried little conviction.

Her mother's smile didn't waver as she stood and gathered her things. "I won't push you," she said gently. "But think about it. You might be surprised by what you find."

As her mother moved toward the kitchen, Jasmine lingered on her phone, scrolling past image after image of unattainable opulence. Yet her mother's words echoed faintly, lingering like a faint melody she couldn't quite shake.

Seeing that her attempts to connect were leading nowhere, her mother stood up, brushing her hands together as if to signal the end of their conversation. She forced a warm smile, masking the tinge of disappointment that shadowed her eyes. "Well," she said, her voice gentle but with an undertone of resignation, "I'll go make some pancakes for breakfast. You used to love those."

Jasmine didn't lift her head, offering only a noncommittal grunt in response. Her attention remained locked on the glowing screen in her hand, her thoughts consumed by the curated glamour and envy-inducing perfection displayed in post after post.

Her mother lingered for a moment, watching her daughter with a quiet sigh before retreating toward the kitchen. She moved slowly, her steps soft, as if to avoid disturbing Jasmine's bubble. The sound of pans clinking faintly carried from the kitchen, followed by the rustle of ingredients being pulled from cabinets— a familiar rhythm of care wrapped in routine.

Jasmine, oblivious to the undercurrent of concern her mother carried, continued scrolling through her feed. A shimmering gown, a private jet, the pristine interior of a luxury home—it was all there, feeding the gnawing ache of longing for a life that felt impossibly out of reach.

Her thumb paused briefly on a photo of a young woman standing on the steps of a yacht, her smile radiant, her caption overflowing with hashtags about success and living one's best life. Jasmine stared, her mind alight with questions she wouldn't say aloud. How did she get there? What's her secret? Will I ever have something like this?

From the kitchen, the faint aroma of butter melting on a skillet wafted into the living room, a comforting reminder of simpler times. But for Jasmine, it went unnoticed, drowned beneath the vivid images of lives that sparkled brighter than her own.

A brief pause filled the room after her mother's departure, the only sound being the faint hum of her phone and the occasional distant clang of pans from the kitchen. Suddenly, the sharp chime of the doorbell cut through the stillness. Jasmine looked up from her screen, visibly irritated by the interruption.

"Who is it?" she called out, her voice carrying a note of annoyance.

Reluctantly, she set her phone down, the weight of disinterest evident in her slow, deliberate movements as she walked toward the door. Her thoughts lingered on the posts she'd been scrolling through, shaping her mood into one of mild exasperation before she even turned the handle.

The door creaked open, revealing a man standing on the threshold, his presence radiating a quiet warmth. He was in his early 30s, neatly dressed, and carried a simple gift box in his hands. His expression held a mixture of hope and nervousness, as though uncertain about the reception he might receive.

"Hi, Jasmine," he said, his voice soft but steady, his smile genuine and disarming.

She gave him a once-over and then rolled her eyes, leaning slightly against the doorframe but making no move to invite him in. "Marcus," she acknowledged flatly, her tone lacking the enthusiasm his arrival seemed to warrant.

He shifted slightly, adjusting his grip on the box, his smile unwavering despite her lukewarm greeting. "I thought I'd drop by," he began, a slight hesitation creeping into his words. "I, uh... brought something for you." He held out the box, its simple wrapping hinting at care rather than extravagance.

Jasmine glanced at it, her eyebrows arching just enough to show mild curiosity. "What's this?" she asked, her tone edging on skeptical.

"A little something I thought you'd like," he replied, his confidence growing as he stepped slightly closer. "I remembered you saying you missed those macarons from that café downtown, so I picked some up for you."

Her expression softened momentarily, though she quickly masked it with indifference. "Macarons?" she repeated, reaching out to take the box. "I guess that's thoughtful."

He chuckled lightly, sensing her walls but choosing not to press. "I hoped it would be," he said. "They had a new flavor, and I thought, 'Jasmine might like this.'"

She opened the box slowly, revealing an assortment of brightly colored macarons nestled in delicate rows. The scent of almond and fruit wafted up, momentarily breaking through her cool exterior.

"Not bad," she murmured, lifting one and inspecting it like a jeweler examining a rare gem. She took a small bite, the crisp shell giving way to a burst of creamy filling. A flicker of satisfaction crossed her face before she quickly suppressed it.

Marcus smiled, watching her reaction. "I'm glad you like them," he said, the warmth in his tone genuine.

Jasmine closed the box with a deliberate motion, setting it on the nearby console table. "So, what brings you here, Marcus?" she asked, crossing her arms as she leaned against the doorframe.

Chapter 2

He rubbed the back of his neck, his nervous energy returning. "Well, I haven't seen you in a while, and I thought it might be nice to catch up. I've been meaning to..." He trailed off, searching for the right words.

She raised an eyebrow, her expression challenging. "Meaning to what?"

"Meaning to see how you've been," he said earnestly, his eyes meeting hers. "It's been a while since we had a proper conversation."

Jasmine gave a half-shrug, her gaze flitting away. "I've been fine," she said vaguely, her tone making it clear she wasn't keen on elaborating.

"Fine doesn't really say much," he countered gently, his smile never faltering. "You've always got more going on than you let on."

She rolled her eyes again, though this time there was less bite to it. "Still the same old Marcus," she said, shaking her head. "Always trying to dig deeper."

He chuckled softly. "And you're still the same Jasmine," he said, his voice carrying a hint of nostalgia. "Always putting up walls."

For a moment, the air between them hung heavy with unspoken history. He glanced past her into the apartment, catching sight of the familiar, cozy living room that felt both welcoming and distant.

"Your mom around?" he asked, changing the subject slightly.

"Yeah, she's in the kitchen," Jasmine replied, stepping aside slightly as if to let him in but not fully committing to the gesture.

"Ah, making her famous pancakes, I bet," he said with a grin.

"How'd you guess?" Jasmine replied, a small smirk tugging at the corner of her lips despite herself.

"She always makes them when she wants to brighten someone's day," he said knowingly.

Jasmine tilted her head, a flicker of something akin to guilt crossing her face. She shrugged it off quickly, though, and motioned toward the couch. "You coming in, or are we having this whole conversation in the doorway?"

He stepped inside, his movements careful, as though navigating uncharted territory. The warmth of the apartment enveloped him, contrasting sharply with the cool detachment Jasmine tried to project.

As he settled onto the couch, she perched on the armrest, keeping a slight distance. He glanced at the coffee table, noting the abandoned cup of coffee and the scattered signs of her morning.

"Busy day, huh?" he remarked lightly, nodding toward the table.

"You could say that," she replied, her tone evasive.

"Anything exciting?" he probed, his tone casual but curious.

She hesitated, then shrugged. "Just... the usual."

"Social media, then?" he guessed, his smile teasing but not unkind.

She narrowed her eyes at him playfully. "What's it to you?"

"Just wondering if it's still as glamorous as it looks," he said, leaning back. "Or if it's starting to feel... hollow."

Her expression faltered for a fraction of a second before she masked it with a smirk. "You always think you're so wise, don't you?"

He laughed softly. "Not wise, just observant," he said. "And maybe a little worried about you."

Jasmine's gaze softened, but she quickly deflected. "You shouldn't be. I'm fine."

Marcus didn't push further, sensing the limits of her willingness to engage. Instead, he leaned forward, resting his elbows on his knees. "Well, how about this—let's make a deal. I bring more macarons next time, and you tell me what's really on your mind. Deal?"

She gave him a skeptical look, then rolled her eyes yet again. "We'll see," she said, her tone light but not dismissive.

Jasmine sighed audibly, her irritation spilling into her tone. "What do you want, Marcus?" she asked, her words clipped as she leaned against the doorframe.

Marcus hesitated for a moment, then offered a shy smile. His hands extended forward, holding out a small, neatly wrapped gift box. "I just wanted to drop this off," he said, his voice calm and hopeful. "I thought you might like it."

Her mother's face briefly appeared in the doorway of the kitchen, curiosity flickering in her eyes as she tried to gauge what was happening. She lingered for a moment before retreating back into the kitchen, the faint sounds of pancakes sizzling returning as the only background noise.

Jasmine took the box, her movements mechanical, offering Marcus a half-hearted smile as though fulfilling a social obligation. Without much interest, she untied the ribbon and opened the lid, revealing a delicate bracelet nestled inside. The small charm attached bore her name engraved in a simple, elegant script.

Marcus watched her closely, his smile warm but tinged with nervous anticipation. "I thought it might be something you'd like," he said softly.

Jasmine examined the bracelet for a moment, her expression unreadable, but then her face shifted. Her features hardened, her lips curving into a displeased frown. She looked up, meeting Marcus's gaze with disappointment written all over her face.

"What is this?" she asked, her tone sharp and unkind.

Marcus blinked, his smile faltering slightly. "It's... it's a bracelet," he explained, his voice steady but uncertain. "I saw it and thought of you."

Her eyes narrowed as she dangled the bracelet in front of him, the delicate chain glinting in the light. "This is cheap, Marcus," she said flatly, her words cutting like glass. "You know I don't wear stuff like this. I need something with a little more... bling."

The warmth in Marcus's face drained, replaced by a quiet embarrassment. He shifted on his feet, rubbing the back of his neck as he tried to muster a response. "I... I thought it was meaningful," he said, his tone subdued. "I didn't mean to—"

Jasmine interrupted him, dropping the bracelet back into the box with an audible clink. "Meaningful doesn't pay the bills, Marcus," she said with a dismissive shrug. "Next time, maybe go for something that actually looks expensive."

Her words hung in the air, heavy and unapologetic. Marcus stood there, silent for a moment, his eyes searching her face for any trace of warmth or understanding. Finding none, he nodded slightly, his expression a mix of hurt and resignation.

"I'm sorry if it's not what you wanted," he said quietly, taking a step back toward the doorway. "I just wanted to do something nice for you."

Jasmine crossed her arms, leaning against the doorframe once more. "Maybe think it through better next time," she said, her tone indifferent.

Jasmine's disdain was palpable as she tossed the bracelet and the box across the room. The small box landed with a dull thud, its contents scattering slightly on the floor. Her tone cut through the air like a knife, sharp and dismissive. "I don't need some meaningless trinket," she said, her voice laced with scorn. "If you want to impress me, you're gonna have to do better than this."

Marcus's expression fell, the hope in his eyes dimming as her words landed. For a moment, he seemed frozen, trying to process the rejection. Despite the clear hurt etched on his face, he managed to force a small, fragile smile. "Jasmine," he began, his voice gentle but tinged with pain, "it's not about the price. It's about what it means—"

She cut him off with a dismissive wave of her hand. "What it means?" she said, her tone mocking. "It means you don't know what I like. It means you think some cheap little bauble is enough to impress me."

Marcus hesitated, the weight of her words pressing down on him. His heart was clearly breaking, but he did his best to maintain composure. "I just wanted to give you something special," he said softly. "But if you don't like it, that's okay. I... I can take it back."

Jasmine scoffed, crossing her arms as she shook her head. Her expression was a mixture of irritation and incredulity. "Yeah, you do that," she said, her words dripping with derision. "And while you're at it, maybe think about stepping up your game, Marcus. I can't be seen with someone who gives out Dollar Store gifts."

Marcus looked down, his smile faltering completely. He nodded slowly, the hurt now fully visible in his eyes. "I understand," he said quietly, his voice barely audible.

For a moment, he lingered, as though hoping she might soften or offer some kind of reassurance. But Jasmine simply turned away, dismissing him entirely as she reached for her phone, already scrolling through her feed as though he wasn't even there.

Realizing there was nothing more to say, Marcus turned and walked out the door, closing it gently behind him. The sound was almost too soft to be noticed, but it echoed in the silence of the room.

Jasmine didn't even glance up, her attention fully absorbed by the glowing screen in her hand. The bracelet lay forgotten on the floor, a stark reminder of the chasm between her world of superficial desires and the genuine kindness Marcus had tried to offer.

In the kitchen, her mother paused in her cooking, her brow furrowed with concern. She had overheard enough to understand what had happened. With a deep sigh, she flipped another pancake, the act both routine and contemplative. The smell of maple syrup and butter filled the air, a faint contrast to the tension lingering in the house.

Marcus held onto the box tightly, his fingers gripping the edges as if it were the only thing grounding him at that moment. His eyes lingered on Jasmine, searching her expression for any hint of warmth or understanding. Instead, he found her gaze steely and indifferent, her stance firm and unyielding.

"I'm sorry you feel that way, Jasmine," he said softly, his voice carrying a weight of sadness. "I just... I just wanted to make you smile."

Jasmine crossed her arms, her expression resolute. "Well," she said, her tone as sharp as a knife, "next time, try harder."

The words hit him like a blow, but Marcus only nodded, as if resigned to her judgment. He stood there for a moment longer, as though hoping she might reconsider, that she might say something—anything—to soften the edges of her cruelty. But Jasmine simply looked at him, unyielding.

Marcus turned slowly, his shoulders slumping under the invisible weight of her rejection. As he walked out, the faint creak of the door and the soft click of it closing behind him felt like the punctuation to a chapter he hadn't wanted to end this way.

In the kitchen, Mrs. Thompson watched the scene unfold from a distance. She clutched a dish towel in her hand, her heart aching as she saw Marcus's defeated posture. She wanted to say something, to offer him comfort or speak to Jasmine about her behavior, but the moment slipped away, and she quietly returned to flipping pancakes.

Jasmine, completely oblivious to the emotional wreckage she'd left in her wake, shut the door with a flip of her hair. There was an air of indifference in her movements as she strolled back to the couch, her phone already in hand before she even sat down.

She flopped onto the cushions, her body sinking lazily into the comfort of the plush fabric. Her fingers found their familiar rhythm against the screen, scrolling through an endless parade of curated lives and unattainable luxuries. The bracelet Marcus had given her didn't cross her mind, forgotten as quickly as it had been dismissed.

Outside, Marcus paused on the sidewalk, staring down at the box in his hand. The bracelet's charm gleamed faintly in the sunlight, a quiet testament to the thought he had put into it. He took a deep breath, his chest rising and falling as he tried to shake off the sting of Jasmine's words. After a moment, he walked away, his pace slow and heavy.

Inside the house, Mrs. Thompson glanced toward the living room, her heart heavy with concern. She wiped her hands on her apron, wondering how to bridge the widening gap between her daughter's shallow pursuits and the deeper values she hoped to instill. The smell of pancakes filled the air, but the sweetness couldn't mask the bitter reality that hung over the house like a cloud.

Jasmine remained on the couch, utterly absorbed in her digital world, completely unaware of the ripple effects of her actions. As she laughed at a video on her feed, the only sounds in the house were the soft sizzle of pancakes in the kitchen and the faint hum of her scrolling phone—a stark contrast to the silence Marcus had left behind.

The door closed with a faint click, leaving Jasmine alone in the room once more. The door closing had marked more than

Marcus's departure; it had sealed another crack in a connection that might never fully mend.

Mrs. Thompson stepped into the living room, her hands carefully balancing a plate piled high with fluffy, golden pancakes. The smell of warm maple syrup wafted through the air as she placed the plate gently on the coffee table in front of her daughter.

"I made your favorite—fluffy pancakes," she said with a warm smile, her voice filled with hope that this small gesture might spark some warmth in Jasmine's mood.

Jasmine barely lifted her eyes from her phone, the bright glow of the screen reflecting in her indifferent gaze. "Yeah, thanks," she muttered, her tone dismissive, fingers still scrolling through her social media feed.

Mrs. Thompson's smile faltered, a subtle flicker of disappointment crossing her face, but she quickly masked it. She smoothed her hands over her lap and sat down beside Jasmine, determined to try again.

"You know," Mrs. Thompson began, her tone light and conversational, "I remember when you were little, you couldn't wait for pancake mornings. You'd sit right there in your pajamas, syrup smeared all over your cheeks, and say they were the best pancakes in the world."

Jasmine smirked faintly, though her eyes remained glued to her phone. "Yeah, well, I guess things change," she said, her voice devoid of nostalgia.

Mrs. Thompson sighed quietly, stealing a glance at the untouched plate. She leaned forward, folding her hands together, searching for a way to connect. "Marcus seemed like a nice young man," she ventured, her voice gentle but probing. "He clearly cares about you, Jasmine. Did you really have to send him away like that?"

Jasmine finally looked up, her brows knitting together in irritation. "Mom, he's just… not my type, okay? I don't need someone who gives me cheap gifts and talks about feelings all the time. I need someone who can actually match my energy, my lifestyle."

Mrs. Thompson frowned, her heart sinking at the shallow words. "Jasmine," she said softly, choosing her words carefully, "life isn't about flashy things or people who can spoil you. It's about connections, about kindness and understanding. Marcus brought you that gift because he thought it would make you happy. That means something."

Jasmine rolled her eyes, setting her phone down with a dramatic sigh. "Mom, you don't get it. People don't notice kindness. They notice style, confidence, success. That's what matters in the real world."

Mrs. Thompson tilted her head, her gaze tender but firm. "And what happens when the style fades, Jasmine? When the success feels empty? What will matter then?"

Jasmine shrugged, her face a mix of frustration and dismissal. "I don't know, Mom. I'll figure it out when I get there."

Mrs. Thompson's shoulders sagged slightly, but she refused to give up. She placed a hand on Jasmine's knee, her touch warm and reassuring. "I just want you to think about what really brings you joy, Jasmine. Not the things that look good on the outside, but the things that fill your heart. The people who genuinely care about you. That's where real happiness comes from."

Jasmine stared at her mother, the words lingering in the air between them. For a moment, something flickered in her expression—uncertainty, perhaps, or the faintest hint of guilt—but it vanished as quickly as it appeared.

"Thanks for the pep talk, Mom," she said flatly, picking up her phone again. "But I'm fine. Really."

Mrs. Thompson sat quietly for a moment, her heart heavy with concern. She reached for the plate of pancakes, taking one for herself and nibbling at the edge. "Well, at least try one," she said softly. "I made them with love, just like always."

Jasmine sighed but reached out, plucking a pancake from the plate and biting into it with a faintly annoyed expression. "Happy now?" she mumbled around a mouthful.

Mrs. Thompson smiled faintly, holding onto the small victory, even if it felt bittersweet. She leaned back, watching her daughter, silently praying for the day Jasmine might truly see the value in the things money couldn't buy.

Mrs. Thompson leaned back in her chair, her voice taking on a casual tone as she said, "So, Marcus stopped by earlier. Why didn't you let your friend in?"

Jasmine lowered her phone slightly, just enough to throw a dismissive glance at her mother before rolling her eyes. "He's not my friend, Mom," she said flatly, her tone sharp enough to make her stance clear.

Mrs. Thompson nodded thoughtfully, as if acknowledging Jasmine's insistence but refusing to let the subject drop entirely. "Okay," she replied, her voice softening with a sigh, "but why didn't you let him in?"

Jasmine shrugged, her focus already back on her phone, fingers tapping away. "It wasn't necessary," she replied, her words as indifferent as her attitude.

Chapter 3

As Mrs. Thompson adjusted her position on the couch, her eyes caught sight of something on the floor. It was the gift Marcus had brought earlier, the delicate bracelet and its box carelessly scattered across the rug. The charm with Jasmine's name etched on it glinted faintly in the sunlight streaming through the window.

Mrs. Thompson's gaze landed on the scattered box and bracelet on the floor. She leaned forward slightly, her expression puzzled. "Who brought that?" she asked, gesturing toward the gift.

Jasmine barely glanced at the item, her face hardening as she muttered coldly, "That low life."

Mrs. Thompson's brows furrowed, a disapproving frown forming on her lips. Her tone carried a note of gentle reprimand as she said, "Jasmine, don't talk about your friend like that."

Jasmine turned to her mother, her expression sharp and unyielding. "He's not my friend," she said tersely, her words cutting like a blade.

Mrs. Thompson straightened up, her eyes narrowing slightly. "He's someone who cares enough to bring you a thoughtful gift," she countered, her voice calm but firm. "That should count for something."

Jasmine scoffed, crossing her arms as she leaned back into the couch. "If he cared so much, he'd bring something worth my time," she snapped. "Not...that." She waved dismissively toward the bracelet, her disdain evident.

Mrs. Thompson sighed deeply, her shoulders sagging with the weight of her disappointment. She bent down to pick up the bracelet, holding it delicately in her hand as she examined the charm with Jasmine's name engraved on it.

"You know," she began softly, her voice almost a whisper, "there are people in this world who would treasure even the simplest gesture of kindness. This wasn't just a gift, Jasmine—it was an effort to make you feel special."

Jasmine looked away, her jaw tightening. "It's not my fault he doesn't know what I like," she said defensively.

Mrs. Thompson shook her head, her eyes reflecting a mix of sadness and frustration. "Maybe it's not about what you like," she said quietly. "Maybe it's about recognizing that someone thought of you. That someone cared enough to try."

For a moment, there was silence between them, the weight of Mrs. Thompson's words hanging in the air. Jasmine shifted uncomfortably, but her expression remained guarded, her walls firmly in place.

Mrs. Thompson placed the bracelet gently on the coffee table and rose to her feet. "Think about it, Jasmine," she said, her voice steady but laced with quiet hope. "Because one day, you might realize that what you're dismissing now is exactly what you'll wish you had more of."

Jasmine glanced up briefly, her expression unreadable. "It's just not my style, Mom," she replied, as if that was all the justification she needed.

Mrs. Thompson held the bracelet in her hand, her thumb brushing over the engraved charm. "It's not about style, Jasmine," she said gently, her eyes lifting to meet her daughter's. "It's about the thought. Marcus didn't have to bring you anything, but he did. That should mean something to you."

Jasmine let out a small scoff, leaning back against the couch. "Mom, people bring gifts all the time. It doesn't mean I have to like them," she said dismissively, her words cutting through the quiet sincerity in her mother's voice.

Mrs. Thompson placed the bracelet carefully on the coffee table, her movements slow and deliberate. "You know," she began, her tone calm but firm, "sometimes it's not about liking the gift. It's about appreciating the effort, the intention behind it. Marcus thought of you when he saw this. That should matter."

Jasmine crossed her arms, her lips pressing into a thin line. "Well, maybe he should think harder next time," she said, her voice cold and unyielding.

Mrs. Thompson studied her daughter for a moment, her heart heavy with a mixture of sadness and frustration. "Jasmine," she said quietly, "do you ever wonder why people go out of their way for you? What they see in you that makes them want to care?"

Jasmine shifted uncomfortably under her mother's gaze, her fingers fidgeting with the edge of her phone case. "I don't know, Mom," she mumbled. "Maybe they shouldn't."

Mrs. Thompson sighed deeply, leaning forward to rest her elbows on her knees. "I just want you to think about it," she said softly, her eyes filled with quiet hope. "The world is already full of people who don't care. Don't push away the ones who do."

For a moment, Jasmine looked at her mother, her expression softening just slightly. But the moment passed as quickly as it came, and she picked up her phone again, her eyes darting back to the screen.

"Yeah, okay," she said absently, her tone signaling the end of the conversation.

Mrs. Thompson gave her a knowing look, the kind that saw through all the bravado Jasmine tried to put up. She spoke softly, almost cautiously. "But he comes by every day..."

Jasmine sighed heavily, an exaggerated display of frustration. She set her phone down on the cushion beside her and met her mother's gaze. "That's because he's a simp," she said flatly, her voice carrying the kind of disdain that made Mrs. Thompson flinch internally.

Mrs. Thompson raised an eyebrow, both surprised and bemused by her daughter's bluntness. "Maybe he likes you," she said suggestively, her tone teasing but also probing.

Jasmine leaned back into the couch, crossing her arms over her chest. Her expression remained detached, almost dismissive. "I don't do men who have nothing, Mom. Remember?" Her words were sharp, cutting through the air like glass.

Mrs. Thompson paused, her playful demeanor melting into one of concern. Her face softened as she took in the guarded expression on her daughter's face. Slowly, she reached out a hand, almost instinctively, to comfort Jasmine. But she stopped halfway, hesitating. There was a wall there, one she wasn't sure how to break through.

She let her hand drop to her lap, her eyes searching Jasmine's face for a glimmer of the daughter she once knew—the one who laughed freely and found joy in the simplest things. "Honey," she began gently, "is it really about what someone has? Or is it about what they can bring into your life, beyond the material things?"

Jasmine's jaw tightened, her gaze fixed somewhere over her mother's shoulder. "It's about not settling, Mom," she said firmly. "I know what I want, and it's not...that."

Mrs. Thompson sighed, her shoulders sinking as if weighed down by the invisible burden of Jasmine's words. "Wanting the best for yourself is one thing," she said quietly. "But dismissing someone's heart because it doesn't come wrapped in glitter... That's something else entirely."

Jasmine shifted in her seat, clearly uncomfortable with the direction the conversation had taken. "Why are you defending him, anyway?" she asked, her tone defensive. "It's not like he's going to change my mind."

Mrs. Thompson gave her a small, sad smile. "I'm not defending him," she said softly. "I'm just reminding you that people who care about us... they're not as common as you think. Sometimes, it's worth looking past the surface to see what's underneath."

The room fell silent for a moment, the weight of Mrs. Thompson's words hanging heavily in the air. Jasmine picked up her phone again, as if to escape the conversation. But her movements were slower this time, her fingers lingering over the screen as if her mother's words had managed to find a crack in her armor.

Mrs. Thompson stood, smoothing her hands over her apron. "I'll be in the kitchen if you need me," she said gently, leaving Jasmine alone with her thoughts and the quiet echo of her own dismissive words.

Her mother gave her a knowing look, speaking softly. "But he comes by every day…"

Jasmine sighed heavily, setting her phone down and looking directly at her. "That's because he's a simp."

Raising an eyebrow, her mother seemed surprised but not entirely unfamiliar with her daughter's bluntness. "Maybe he likes you," she said, her tone suggestive.

Leaning back, arms crossed, Jasmine wore an indifferent expression. "I don't do men who have nothing, Mom. Remember?"

The room seemed to fall silent for a moment. Her mother paused, her face softening with concern. She reached out as if to comfort her daughter but hesitated, unsure how to bridge the gap between them. Finally, she spoke again, her voice firmer this time. "It's not always about what they have, you know. Sometimes, it's about who they are."

Jasmine rolled her eyes, her tone sharp. "Well, who they are isn't going to pay for my dream life, is it?"

Her mother frowned, her patience thinning. "What about Kevin? Nice young man, doing well for himself."

"Kevin?" Jasmine snorted, her laughter cold and dismissive. "Mom, please. He's so broke, he can barely afford a second shirt. How am I supposed to be seen with him?"

A sigh escaped her mother, but she pressed on. "Well, what about Brandon? He's got his own business. People around here speak highly of him."

"Brandon?" Jasmine repeated, rolling her eyes again. "No one even knows him in this community, let alone outside it. How's he supposed to make me famous?"

Her mother's brow furrowed slightly, but she refused to give up. "And Charles? He's been a faithful churchgoer for years. Always respectful…"

"Charles?" Jasmine interrupted, her voice laced with disdain. "Mom, he's short and dark. I'm not interested in someone who looks like that."

Her mother folded her arms across her chest, exasperation flashing in her eyes. She took a deep breath, steadying her tone. "Jasmine, you can't dismiss people based on such shallow reasons. Life isn't about looks or fame."

A sharp laugh escaped Jasmine's lips as she slouched back into the couch. "Oh, here we go. The life lessons. Let me guess—next, you're going to tell me it's about what's on the inside, not the outside, right?"

Her mother's lips pressed into a thin line as she leaned forward slightly, her voice calm but firm. "It is about what's on the inside. And you know that deep down. Look at Marcus—he shows up every day, trying to bring a little light into your life. But you treat him like he's invisible."

Jasmine slumped further into her seat, her expression unreadable. "Marcus isn't invisible, Mom. He's just... irrelevant."

Her mother's frown deepened, the weight of the words clearly affecting her. She took a seat beside Jasmine, leaning closer. "Why do you talk like this? When did everything become about how much money someone has, or how they look, or how famous they are?"

Jasmine shifted uncomfortably, her tone defensive. "I'm not settling, Mom. I deserve better. Why should I waste my time on someone who can't give me the life I want?"

Her mother's gaze softened, her voice dropping to a near whisper. "But what do you want? Is it a life full of expensive things and empty conversations? Or do you want someone who's going to stand by you, love you, and make you feel valued?"

For a moment, Jasmine hesitated. The silence hung between them, heavy with unspoken truths. Then, her walls came back up, and her tone turned cold again. "I want a life where I don't have to struggle like you and Dad did."

Her mother winced, straightening her posture. "Your father and I didn't struggle because we didn't have money. We struggled because we wanted to give you and your siblings the best we could. We didn't measure success by bank accounts or fancy cars. We measured it by the love in this home."

Jasmine stared ahead, her jaw tight, refusing to meet her mother's eyes. "Love doesn't pay the bills," she muttered under her breath.

Her mother shook her head slowly, the hurt visible in her expression. "No, but love builds a life. Money comes and goes, but the people who care for you... they're the ones who stay."

The words seemed to linger in the air, but Jasmine said nothing. She grabbed her phone again, scrolling aimlessly, signaling the end of the conversation.

Her mother stood, brushing her hands against her apron as though trying to shake off the heaviness. She paused at the doorway, glancing over her shoulder one last time. Her voice was soft but carried a weight that pierced the silence. "And sometimes, you don't realize who truly cares for you until they're gone."

Jasmine's fingers hovered over her phone, her scrolling slowing down as a flicker of uncertainty crossed her face. She quickly shook it off, retreating once more into the comforting distraction of her screen.

Mrs. Thompson sat in her favorite armchair, her eyes narrowing as she studied her daughter, Jasmine. The living room was quiet, the kind of stillness that only came when everything else seemed to be in place. The old grandfather clock in the corner ticked steadily, a sound that felt unusually loud against the silence. Mrs. Thompson had noticed something off about Jasmine's tone earlier, a certain sharpness that hinted at something deeper. She had spent the last few weeks pondering over her daughter's growing detachment, wondering if it was just a phase or something more.

After a long pause, Mrs. Thompson cleared her throat, her voice laced with a motherly concern that hadn't changed since the day Jasmine was born. "So," she began slowly, carefully choosing her words, "what kind of man are you looking for, Jasmine?"

The question hung in the air, heavy with the weight of years of life lessons, hopes, and dreams. Mrs. Thompson had always hoped her daughter would find someone who could make her happy—not just a rich man, but someone who could offer her love, respect, and a sense of security. She had seen enough of the world to know that those were the things that truly mattered in a marriage. But Jasmine... Jasmine had always been a different breed—ambitious, headstrong, and determined to carve her own path, even if that path sometimes seemed a little too focused on the material.

Jasmine sat up straighter, her posture immediately shifting as if the question had riled something inside her. She looked over at her mother, a faint smirk playing on her lips, almost like she was amused by the very thought. Jasmine had always been confident, but today, there was something even more resolute in her eyes, something that gave Mrs. Thompson pause.

With a soft chuckle, Jasmine leaned back slightly in her chair, her fingers tracing the rim of her coffee cup absentmindedly. "Tall, fair, rich, and famous," she said, her tone almost flippant, but sharp as a knife. "A man who's known all over the world, not just some small-town nobody. He has to have everything—money, status, looks. I don't want to settle for anything less."

Mrs. Thompson blinked, taken aback by the response. She had expected something, but not this. Her brow furrowed, a deepening crease forming between her eyes as she took in what Jasmine had just said. The words felt almost rehearsed, as though Jasmine had said them to herself a hundred times before, each time with more certainty than the last.

"You're serious, aren't you?" Mrs. Thompson murmured, her voice quieter now, tinged with disbelief. She leaned forward, resting her elbows on her knees as she studied her daughter more closely. The young woman sitting before her was no longer the little girl who used to cling to her side. Jasmine had grown, changed, become someone she was still trying to understand. But this? This was a side of her that Mrs. Thompson hadn't seen before.

Jasmine met her gaze, her smirk widening just a little. She could see the concern in her mother's eyes, the mixture of confusion and worry. And yet, there was no hesitation in her own heart. Jasmine had made up her mind, and she wasn't about to back down now.

"Why settle for less, Mom?" Jasmine said, her voice firm now, almost challenging. "I've worked hard for everything I have. I've got my own goals, my own ambitions. And why shouldn't I expect the same from the person I choose to spend my life with? A man who's been through the same grind, who's made something of himself. You know, the kind of man who doesn't just sit around in some little town, waiting for life to hand him something. I want a man who's seen the world, who's got experience, who's lived it all and come out on top."

Mrs. Thompson's heart sank a little. She had raised Jasmine to be strong, independent, and capable of achieving anything she set her mind to. But there was something about this new version of Jasmine that made her uneasy. It was as though her daughter was no longer interested in the simple things—things like love, companionship, or building a life together. Instead, Jasmine seemed fixated on the external markers of success: wealth, fame, and status.

"You think money and fame will bring happiness?" Mrs. Thompson asked, her voice softer now, tinged with a mix of sadness and concern. She could feel the years of experience in her words. "I've seen enough to know that those things can be fleeting. A person with all the money in the world can still feel empty inside. And fame? It's a double-edged sword, darling. It can lift you up one day and tear you down the next."

Jasmine's smile faltered for a brief moment, but she quickly recovered, shrugging as if to dismiss her mother's words. "I'm not saying I want him to be perfect, Mom. But I want someone who can match me. Someone who can challenge me, push me to be better. Someone who's got the world at his feet, not just some man trying to make ends meet." Her eyes sparkled with an intensity that made Mrs. Thompson feel like she was staring into a mirror, but one that reflected a version of Jasmine she wasn't sure she recognized.

"But what about love, Jasmine?" Mrs. Thompson asked gently, her voice quivering slightly. "What about finding someone who cares for you, someone who sees you for who you are and not just what you can bring to the table? I know you want someone with ambition, but what about someone who has heart? The kind of man who would hold your hand through the hard times, who would be there for you when the world isn't watching?"

Jasmine's expression softened for a moment, as if considering her mother's words. But then, she shook her head, the smirk returning to her lips. "Love is great, Mom. But love doesn't pay the bills. Love doesn't buy you the life you want. I've got dreams, big ones. I need a partner who shares those dreams, not someone who's going to drag me down with his small-town mentality."

Chapter 4

Mrs. Thompson sat back in her chair, her hands clasped tightly in her lap. She could feel the frustration building inside her, but she was determined not to show it. She had spent years teaching Jasmine to be independent, but somewhere along the way, it seemed like her daughter had forgotten the importance of balance. Ambition was important, but so was love. So was the quiet moments of life that no amount of fame or fortune could ever replace.

"I just want you to be careful, darling," Mrs. Thompson said finally, her voice soft but firm. "The world isn't always as glittery as it seems. You don't want to end up chasing something that will leave you empty inside."

Jasmine stood up, her eyes still gleaming with a mix of determination and impatience. "Don't worry about me, Mom. I know what I'm doing." She paused for a moment, glancing back at her mother with a small, almost teasing smile. "Besides, I'm not looking for advice. I'm just letting you know what I want. You'll see. One day, I'll have everything I've dreamed of."

With that, Jasmine turned and walked out of the room, leaving her mother sitting in silence. Mrs. Thompson sat there for a long time after, her thoughts swirling around the conversation, wondering if she had said the right things, if she had done enough to help her daughter understand what truly mattered in life. But deep down, she knew it wasn't about advice anymore. Jasmine had made up her mind. All she could do now was hope that, in the end, her daughter would find what she was truly searching for—whatever that might be.

Mrs. Thompson remained frozen in place, her eyes locked on the doorway where her daughter had just stormed out. The words Jasmine had spoken echoed in her mind, a jarring reminder of the gulf between them, a gulf that seemed to widen with every passing day. She had never imagined it would come to this—a time when her own daughter, the girl she had raised with so much love and care, would turn her back on everything Mrs. Thompson believed in. The principles of kindness, integrity, and love had always been the foundation of their relationship, but now Jasmine seemed to have cast them aside in favor of a life filled with superficial desires.

Mrs. Thompson's gaze dropped to the table in front of her, where a half-eaten stack of pancakes sat untouched, the syrup slowly congealing, no longer glistening. A soft sigh escaped her lips as she reached for her mug of coffee, only to set it down again, her fingers trembling slightly. How had it all come to this? When had her little girl, the one who used to sit on her lap with wide-eyed wonder, asking about the world and dreaming of making a difference, transformed into this version of herself?

The silence in the room felt suffocating now, louder than any argument or raised voice. It wasn't the first time Jasmine had been so dismissive—there had been other moments over the past few months, little cracks in their relationship that had deepened over time. But this… this felt like a final blow.

She blinked back the tears threatening to spill, not wanting to cry, not wanting to show weakness. But the sadness—the raw ache—was undeniable. Jasmine was her daughter, the person she had raised, and yet she couldn't shake the feeling that they were no longer on the same path, no longer in sync. What had happened to the girl who once sought her advice, the one who admired her strength, her values?

"Jasmine..." Mrs. Thompson whispered again, her voice a soft, almost broken sound. It was as if saying her daughter's name one more time might somehow bring her back, or at least make sense of this growing divide.

She heard the heavy thud of footsteps retreating down the hallway, the slam of a door echoing through the house. Mrs. Thompson knew better than to chase after her. Jasmine was far beyond listening now. The conversation had ended, and all Mrs. Thompson could do was wait—wait for the storm to pass, for the anger to dissipate, and for the inevitable regret that always followed a heated argument.

As Mrs. Thompson sat there, lost in thought, she remembered the days when Jasmine was a little girl, her eyes bright with curiosity and hope. Back then, she had dreamed of a future that was full of meaning, not just wealth or status. She had believed that happiness could be found in the simplest moments—like sitting together at the breakfast table, sharing stories, laughing over pancakes. But now, those moments felt like distant memories, fading with each passing day.

Mrs. Thompson closed her eyes for a moment, trying to gather her thoughts, but the truth was hard to ignore. She wasn't sure if Jasmine could ever find her way back to the values she once held dear. Maybe the world had changed too much. Maybe Jasmine had changed too much. Or maybe, just maybe, Mrs. Thompson had failed in some way to instill the right lessons.

With a deep, shuddering breath, she pushed herself to her feet and moved toward the kitchen. She mechanically began clearing the table, her hands moving as if they had a mind of their own. The pancakes remained cold, the syrup now a sticky residue that she wiped away with a cloth. It was a futile task, she knew. The real mess couldn't be cleaned with a dish rag.

She glanced toward the hallway, where Jasmine had disappeared. A fleeting thought crossed her mind—maybe, just maybe, there was a way to fix this. A way to reach her daughter before it was too late. But deep down, she feared that she might already be too late.

Mrs. Thompson sank into a chair by the kitchen table, her shoulders sagging. Her heart felt heavy, weighed down by the overwhelming realization that Jasmine had already chosen her path. And it was one that, in her eyes, could only lead to disappointment.

The door to Jasmine's room was firmly shut, and Mrs. Thompson sat in the stillness, knowing that no matter what she said or did, the chasm between them had grown too wide for a simple conversation to bridge.

Her eyes fell on the untouched breakfast, and for the first time, she wasn't sure if she wanted to finish it. Everything felt empty now.

Mrs. Thompson's voice cracked, desperation creeping into her words as she called out into the silence of the house. Her eyes darted toward the hallway, as though expecting Jasmine to come back, to somehow hear the pain in her mother's voice and reconsider. But the sound of the slamming door still rang in her ears, a painful reminder of the distance that now lay between them.

"Jasmine!" she called again, louder this time, her voice trembling with a mixture of anger and hurt. "Jasmine, don't walk out on me like this!"

But the hallway remained eerily quiet. No response. Not even a sound of footsteps.

Mrs. Thompson stood there for a moment, her breath shallow, her heart pounding in her chest. A knot of frustration twisted in her stomach. She had always told Jasmine that walking away from a conversation, from a problem, would never solve anything. That running from the truth only made it harder to face in the end.

Yet now, here she was, standing alone in the kitchen, her daughter's stubbornness and refusal to listen hanging heavily in the air. It was as if Jasmine had built up an emotional wall—one that Mrs. Thompson couldn't climb over, no matter how hard she tried.

The mother's fingers tightened around the edge of the counter, and for a brief moment, she considered going after Jasmine—knocking on her door, forcing her to listen, demanding some kind of explanation. But she knew, deep down, that it wouldn't work. Jasmine was too angry, too set in her ways. And no matter how much Mrs. Thompson tried to fight it, she realized that pushing too hard might only push her daughter further away.

Her gaze wandered back to the table, the untouched pancakes still sitting there in their sad, half-hearted form. The moment had been so simple, so innocent just moments before. A typical Sunday breakfast. But now it felt like the beginning of something much darker. Something that Mrs. Thompson didn't know how to stop.

The thought of Jasmine, her only child, so full of promise and potential, throwing away everything she had been taught—the values of love, honesty, and hard work—cut through her like a knife. What had happened to the girl who once clung to her every word? Where had that Jasmine gone?

The silence in the house deepened, and Mrs. Thompson realized, with a painful clarity, that she didn't know the answer. Maybe she never had.

Her mind raced, searching for something she could do, anything she could say to fix this. But it felt as if she had run out of time. The gap between them had widened with every harsh word, with every ignored plea, until now it felt as though there was nothing left but empty space.

She felt a tear slip down her cheek, but she quickly wiped it away, not wanting to be weak in front of Jasmine, even though she felt like her whole world was falling apart.

"Jasmine," she whispered again, her voice breaking. "Please, don't shut me out."

The house, once full of the hum of daily life, now seemed hollow, as if it, too, felt the absence of the connection they once shared. Mrs. Thompson sank into the nearest chair, her hands trembling as she held her head in her hands.

What had gone wrong? How had she failed her daughter so completely?

The questions lingered in the air, unanswered and painful, as the sound of Jasmine's retreating footsteps faded away completely.

The room is dimly lit, with the soft hum of her phone the only sound breaking the silence. Jasmine lies sprawled across her bed, her long hair cascading over the pillow as she absently scrolls through her phone, her eyes half-lidded with boredom. She shifts a little, her fingers swiping lazily, as if the world around her is unremarkable. The glow from the phone's screen casts an eerie light on her face, highlighting the cool indifference in her expression.

Suddenly, a ping breaks the monotony. Her fingers hover over the phone, her interest piqued, and she taps the screen to reveal the message.

(ON THE SCREEN) Sarah: "House party at Stacy's tonight. Big people will be there. Make sure you look sexy ☺. Starts at 10 PM. Don't be late!"

Jasmine's lips curve into a smirk as she reads the message, her eyes gleaming with a mix of amusement and anticipation. She glances over at her reflection in the mirror for a moment, then lets out a breath, her smirk widening.

"Big people, huh?" she murmurs to herself, her tone laced with self-assurance.

She tosses the phone aside with a casual flick of her wrist, the device bouncing on the bed before coming to a stop. The moment is fleeting, as her mind is already moving on to the next step.

With a practiced ease, she rolls off the bed, her feet hitting the soft carpeted floor. Standing up, she glances around her room, the chaos of clothing scattered across the floor, shoes haphazardly thrown around. It's a mess, but she pays it no mind. Her focus is on what's to come—the party, the people, and the image she's about to create.

Jasmine walks to her closet, the door sliding open with a soft whoosh. Her eyes flick over the clothing racks, scanning each outfit with a critical gaze. She pulls a few things out, holding them up against her body in the mirror, evaluating each one. A black leather jacket? Too edgy. A tight red dress? Too obvious.

Finally, she lands on something that catches her eye—a figure-hugging silver sequined dress, sleek and flashy, something that screams confidence. The kind of outfit that doesn't just get noticed—it demands it.

Jasmine steps into the dress, the fabric shimmering against her skin as she zips it up with practiced ease. She examines herself in the mirror, her lips curling into a satisfied smile. The dress fits her perfectly, accentuating every curve in all the right ways. She twirls once in front of the mirror, watching as the sequins catch the light, casting a sparkle around the room.

"Perfect," she says, as if confirming her own success. She grabs a pair of stilettos from the floor, slipping them on effortlessly, her gaze never leaving the mirror.

She adjusts her hair, a few strands falling into place, and then turns to her makeup table. Jasmine applies a bold layer of lipstick, the rich red shade contrasting sharply with her fair skin. Her eyes glint with mischief as she picks up the eyeliner, giving herself a sharp cat-eye look, adding the final touch to her transformation.

With a satisfied nod, she steps back, admiring herself one last time before heading toward the door. The clock on the wall reads 9:30 PM.

"Not bad," she mutters to herself, her voice tinged with excitement. She grabs her phone off the bed, checking for any last-minute updates. Nothing new. Perfect.

As she heads toward the door, a sense of anticipation builds in her chest. Tonight isn't just any night. Tonight, she'll be seen. Tonight, she'll be the one everyone talks about.

The heavy bass of music vibrates through the floor as Jasmine and Sarah step into the house, immediately swallowed by the sounds of laughter, chatter, and clinking glasses. The party is already in full swing. The air is thick with the scent of expensive perfume, alcohol, and the faint, lingering smell of a burning candle somewhere in the distance. The walls are adorned with extravagant decorations: velvet drapes, shimmering fairy lights, and an oversized chandelier that casts a soft, golden glow over the guests, its light flickering like fireflies in the night.

The room is packed with people—well-dressed men and women engaged in animated conversations, most holding drinks in their hands, others swaying to the rhythm of the music. Everyone seems to know someone, and the sense of exclusivity is palpable. The kind of party where being a part of the inner circle means you're in the right place, at the right time, with the right people.

Jasmine and Sarah, both dressed in eye-catching outfits that leave little to the imagination, make their way through the crowd. Jasmine's silver sequined dress clings to her body like a second skin, the sequins glinting under the soft lighting with every step she takes. The dress is a statement—a shimmering beacon of confidence and allure. Her hair falls in loose waves over her shoulders, and her bold makeup—dark eyeliner, crimson lips—gives her a striking, almost otherworldly look.

Sarah, beside her, isn't far behind in the fashion department. She's wearing a tight, strapless black dress with a plunging neckline that shows off her curves. She grins, her eyes scanning the room with excitement as she gestures for Jasmine to follow her toward the bar. The party's energy is contagious, and both of them feel the rush of adrenaline building in their veins.

"I swear, Jasmine, this place is on fire tonight," Sarah says, her voice barely audible over the music, her excitement evident in her wide grin. "I can already spot a few guys who'll be all over us in no time."

Jasmine's lips curl into a smirk, her eyes scanning the crowd for the "big people" Sarah had mentioned earlier. The type of people who command attention the moment they walk into a room. She knows she'll have no trouble standing out. Tonight, she's going to own this place.

But just as they begin to weave through the crowd, her phone buzzes in her hand, vibrating against her palm. Jasmine pulls it out without much thought, expecting another message or perhaps a notification about the party. Instead, her eyes widen briefly when she sees the caller ID. It's her mom.

Jasmine's finger hovers over the screen, the name Mom flashing in front of her like an unwelcome reminder. Her brows furrow slightly, and for a split second, the weight of the situation begins to settle over her like a heavy fog. But she quickly shakes it off, dismissing the thought as quickly as it came.

She flicks her wrist, turning the phone face down, deciding to ignore it for now.

"Not now," she mutters under her breath, her voice tinged with impatience.

Sarah, noticing Jasmine's distraction, raises an eyebrow. "Everything okay?" she asks, leaning in slightly.

Jasmine glances at her, trying to mask the brief flicker of concern in her eyes. "Yeah, it's just... my mom." She rolls her eyes dramatically, as if the thought of her mother calling is the most insignificant thing in the world. "She probably wants to remind me to be home by midnight or something. Like that's ever going to happen."

Sarah laughs, the sound high-pitched and carefree. "Honestly, you're way too grown up for her to still be on your case like that. You're living your best life, Jas. Let's just enjoy tonight."

Jasmine forces a smile, but deep down, a small part of her is still tugged by the thought of her mom. She quickly silences the nagging feeling and shoves her phone back into her purse, the soft buzz of the vibration still lingering in her mind.

For the next few moments, the party takes over. Jasmine's attention shifts back to the people around her—the flirtatious glances, the subtle touches, the high-pitched laughter filling the air. It's all part of the dance she's learned to master: playing the game, knowing when to smile, when to laugh, when to be the center of attention, and when to hold back.

Chapter 5

Sarah pulls her toward a group of guys near the bar. They all look at Jasmine and Sarah with immediate interest, their eyes lingering just a little longer than they should. One of the men, tall and muscular with perfectly styled hair, leans in and offers a drink to Jasmine.

"Can I get you something, beautiful?" he asks with a grin that speaks more of confidence than actual charm.

Jasmine meets his gaze, not flinching, not breaking her smile. "Just a vodka, neat," she says smoothly, her tone laced with a hint of flirtation. "Make it quick."

Sarah watches the interaction closely, nudging Jasmine with her elbow. "You've got this, girl. They're eating out of your hand."

Jasmine takes the drink without missing a beat, her fingers brushing against the man's as she accepts it. Her eyes meet his for a brief moment, and she knows the game has begun. She's playing it well—better than anyone else in the room.

But even as the night unfurls around her, with every laugh, every glance, every drink, something tugs at the back of Jasmine's mind. It's her mom's call. The message she's been avoiding all evening.

But as she clinks her glass against Sarah's, a toast to a night of excitement and promises unspoken, Jasmine pushes the thought away. Tonight isn't about anything other than herself.

The pulsating beat of the music vibrates through the floor, as if the entire house is alive with the rhythm. The bass thuds in time with Jasmine's heartbeat, an irresistible force that pulls her deeper into the party's chaos. The living room is a swirl of people, the energy electric, the air thick with excitement and the scent of luxury. Groups are scattered around, lounging on plush couches in deep conversation or laughing over drinks. Some are swaying to the music in the center of the room, lost in the rhythm, their bodies moving as one.

The neon lights above the bar flicker, casting multicolored glows that pulse in sync with the beat. The bar itself is a modern spectacle, its countertops glistening under the lights, stocked with every kind of alcohol imaginable. People are gathered there, some leaning in close, others throwing their heads back in laughter, their voices rising above the music as they chat. The smell of expensive cologne and perfume fills the air, sharp and heady, mixing with the scent of alcohol and sweat—a perfume of indulgence, excess, and the promise of a night to remember.

Jasmine and Sarah make their way through the crowd, their outfits a sharp contrast to the sea of people, both dressed to stand out. Jasmine's silver sequined dress sparkles like a thousand tiny stars, catching the light with every movement. Her body moves with purpose, her gaze unwavering as she surveys the party around her. Sarah, equally striking in her black strapless dress, walks just behind her, grinning at the scene in front of them.

As they pass by groups of partygoers, heads turn, eyes lingering a little too long, admiration and curiosity clear on their faces. The air seems to part for them as they glide through the crowd, their presence undeniable.

Jasmine can feel the stares, the whispers, the silent approval of everyone around them. It's like she's the star of her own show, and the spotlight is always on her. She catches a few men looking her way, their gazes not subtle, but she doesn't mind. If anything, it fuels her ego, feeds the fire inside her.

The sound of Sarah's voice pulls her back to the present.

"Oh my…!" Jasmine exclaims, her voice carrying a mix of surprise and delight as she surveys the scene.

Sarah laughs beside her, leaning in closer to shout over the music. "Beats your imagination, right?" she says, her voice full of excitement and admiration.

Jasmine, however, remains unshaken. She tilts her head slightly, her lips curling into a confident, almost arrogant smirk. "I actually expected this," she says with cool nonchalance, her tone laced with self-assurance. There's no doubt in her mind that this party, this crowd, this energy, is exactly what she anticipated. She's been to enough events like this to know what to expect, to know how to walk into a room and own it.

Jasmine's confidence is her shield, her weapon. She steps further into the room, her heels clicking against the polished floor, adding to the rhythm of the music, as if her very presence is part of the beat. She takes in the scene again—people laughing, some chatting quietly in corners, others dancing, letting go. She glances toward the bar, eyeing the mix of familiar and unfamiliar faces there. A few well-known names from her school days are perched on stools, laughing with a couple of older men. She wonders if anyone recognizes her from before—if anyone remembers the quiet, reserved girl she used to be. But she brushes the thought away quickly. She's not that girl anymore. Not tonight.

Sarah pulls her attention back, her voice full of excitement. "Okay, let's grab a drink, and then I want to show you the VIP area. There's someone there who might be just your type."

Jasmine raises an eyebrow, intrigued. She's heard that line before, but Sarah has always had a way of finding the right people for the right moment.

"I'm listening," Jasmine says, her tone playful but tinged with curiosity. She flicks her hair over her shoulder as they make their way toward the bar. A few people eye them as they pass, their gaze lingering, but Jasmine doesn't care. She's used to it. She's the one in control here. The night is hers for the taking, and she knows exactly what to do with it.

At the bar, the bartender, a tall, handsome man with a tight smile, catches Jasmine's eye immediately. His gaze lingers a little longer than necessary as he approaches.

"What can I get you?" he asks, his voice smooth and confident, the hint of a flirtation hanging in the air.

Jasmine meets his eyes, her gaze steady and knowing. She leans forward slightly, the movement deliberate, and her lips curl into a playful smile. "A vodka martini. Extra dry," she says, her voice low, smooth.

The bartender nods, seemingly impressed, and starts preparing the drink. Jasmine feels Sarah beside her, watching with an amused smile.

"Seems like you've already got him wrapped around your finger," Sarah teases, nudging Jasmine playfully.

Jasmine smirks again, her gaze still on the bartender as she replies with a casual confidence, "It's just what I do."

The glass is placed in front of her, and Jasmine accepts it without hesitation, her fingers brushing against the bartender's as she takes the drink. She brings it to her lips, taking a slow sip, savoring the cool burn of the alcohol.

Tonight, she tells herself. Tonight, it all begins.

Jasmine's gaze locks onto him instantly, her eyes narrowing slightly as she takes in the sight. He's exactly what she's been looking for—tall, striking, effortlessly stylish. His presence in the room is magnetic, drawing people in without him even trying. She watches him for a moment longer, studying the way he carries himself, the way the group around him seems to defer to his every word.

His fair skin almost glows under the soft, seductive lighting of the room, and the designer shirt he wears seems to fit him like a glove, hugging his broad shoulders and sculpted chest. There's something about the way he moves—slow, deliberate, with a confidence that can't be faked. It's not just his looks; it's his entire aura, the way he commands attention without lifting a finger. Jasmine can already tell he's the kind of man who knows what he wants, and he won't settle for anything less.

"Who's that?" Jasmine's voice is soft, almost to herself, but Sarah hears her. She follows Jasmine's gaze across the room, and her eyes widen with recognition.

"That's Max Donovan," Sarah says, her tone dropping slightly, as if mentioning his name gives him a certain weight. "He's a big deal—comes from money, but he's made a name for himself too. They say he's got a whole empire in the making. The kind of guy who doesn't need to try. He just is."

Jasmine's lips curl into a small, knowing smile. Perfect.

"Well, he certainly looks the part," Jasmine murmurs, her voice taking on an almost imperceptible hint of satisfaction. She takes a step forward, her heels clicking against the floor as she pushes through the crowd, Sarah trailing just behind her.

As they move closer, Jasmine feels the intensity of the room shift. It's like the air itself thickens, and every step she takes brings her closer to something she knows she can't afford to miss. She's always been drawn to power—whether it's in the form of money, status, or sheer presence—and this man has it all.

Max, meanwhile, is unaware of the two women approaching. He's laughing with his friends, enjoying the moment, but his posture remains relaxed, casual. His smile is easy, but there's a glint in his eyes that suggests he's always calculating, always thinking, always in control.

Jasmine finally reaches the table, and as she nears, she's aware of the way people around her subtly part, as if creating a path for her. She doesn't need to look at anyone—she knows she has their attention, and she's not afraid to use it.

As if on cue, Max's eyes flicker up from his conversation. His gaze immediately locks with hers, and for a brief moment, time seems to stop. Jasmine's heartbeat quickens as their eyes meet. She doesn't break the connection, instead holding his gaze with a steady confidence that tells him she's not just any woman in the room—she's the one. His lips curl into a slight, approving smile, the corners of his mouth twitching as if he's been waiting for this moment.

Sarah, sensing the shift in the energy, raises her brows and nudges Jasmine with a knowing grin. "Looks like he's noticed you," she says, her voice low.

Jasmine doesn't respond at first, still watching Max. She feels a surge of excitement, but it's more than just his looks—it's the way he carries himself, the way he's everything she's ever wanted in a man. The idea of having him, of making him hers, feels like the ultimate prize. She feels a strange sense of power in the moment.

Max leans back slightly in his chair, breaking eye contact briefly to scan her outfit. His eyes flick back to hers, an unspoken challenge in his gaze, as if he's daring her to take the next step.

Jasmine smiles, a slow, confident curve of her lips. She tilts her head slightly to the side, taking another sip of her drink, never breaking eye contact. Her body language is open, inviting, but there's an edge to it—something that says she's in control of the situation, not him. She lets the tension build between them, enjoying the thrill of the chase, the magnetic pull that draws them together.

Max finally stands, his movements smooth and effortless, like a lion rising from its rest. He steps toward her, his eyes never leaving hers. The room around them seems to fade as he crosses the distance between them, the music and chatter blurring into the background.

"Jasmine, right?" His voice is deep, calm, but there's an edge to it, a confidence that matches the way he carries himself. His hand extends toward her, and Jasmine takes it, her grip firm and deliberate.

"That's right," she replies, her voice dripping with a mix of warmth and authority. "I've heard a lot about you, Max."

Max raises an eyebrow, intrigued but not surprised. He's used to being the subject of rumors and whispers. But there's something about Jasmine's presence that feels different. She's not like the others—the women who fawn over him, who throw themselves at his feet. She's sharp, calculating, and confident in a way that makes her stand out.

"Well, I hope it was all good things," Max says, his smirk never faltering as he eyes her, intrigued by the challenge she presents.

Jasmine's smile deepens, a subtle hint of mischief dancing in her eyes. "Let's just say… I'm intrigued. I'm curious to know if the reality matches the reputation."

Max chuckles, his laughter low and genuine. "I like that. You're not afraid to test the waters."

Jasmine leans in just slightly, her voice dropping to a softer, more intimate tone. "I never settle for anything less than the best."

The words hang in the air between them, charged with meaning. Max's eyes narrow slightly, but the smile never leaves his lips. He's amused, intrigued, and clearly interested in what she's offering.

"Well, Jasmine," he says, his voice a low drawl, "I think we might just be able to make that happen."

The conversation hangs in the air, thick with unspoken promises, the beginning of a game that neither of them is willing to lose. The energy in the room shifts, the focus now entirely on the two of them as they stand there, locked in a quiet but intense moment of mutual recognition.

Jasmine's heart races, but her exterior remains calm, poised, and in control. She knows this game. She knows how to win.

Jasmine whispered to herself, feeling a rush of excitement as her eyes scanned the room. He's perfect. Exactly what I wanted.

She took a deep breath, steadying her nerves, her gaze fixed on the man across the room. There he was—tall, fair, effortlessly cool, dressed in a crisp designer shirt that clung to his well-toned frame. His posture was relaxed, the kind of self-assurance that oozed from his every movement. Jasmine couldn't help but feel a twinge of admiration. This was the kind of man she had always dreamed of— tall, handsome, rich, and unattainably cool.

Her breath caught in her throat as she watched him interact with his friends, laughing easily, his smile full of confidence. Jasmine couldn't tear her eyes away from him. The noise of the party around her seemed to fade as she zeroed in on him, her mind racing with thoughts of how to catch his attention.

This is it, she thought. This is what I've been waiting for.

"Sarah," she whispered, glancing at her friend beside her. "I'm going to talk to him."

Sarah gave her a playful grin, her eyes glancing toward the man who had captured Jasmine's attention. "I thought you might," she said, voice teasing. "But good luck, though. He doesn't exactly go for girls who throw themselves at him."

Jasmine raised an eyebrow, a confident smile playing on her lips. "I'm not throwing myself at anyone, Sarah. I play the game— and I win."

Sarah laughed, shaking her head, but Jasmine didn't pay her much attention. Her focus was entirely on the man across the room, and with each step she took toward him, her confidence grew. She straightened her posture, her heels clicking against the floor, each step deliberate, her eyes never straying from her target.

As she moved closer, she could feel the weight of his gaze on her. It was as if everything around her paused, the beat of the music growing distant. She could almost feel the air shift between them, the tension mounting. And just as she reached his group, he glanced up, meeting her gaze with a flicker of curiosity. His eyes locked onto hers, and she felt a rush of adrenaline flood her body.

This is it. Time to make my move, she thought, her heart pounding in her chest.

With a slow, deliberate motion, she approached him, allowing the moment to stretch out in the silence between them. She wasn't just another face in the crowd. She was the crowd.

As she stopped in front of him, she let her lips curve into a confident, teasing smile. "Well, I was starting to think I'd never get a chance to meet you."

He raised an eyebrow, a smirk tugging at the corner of his mouth, his interest piqued. He straightened in his seat, his presence commanding. There was a quiet challenge in his eyes, and Jasmine could feel it. She wasn't here to play it safe; she was here to take control.

He didn't respond immediately, letting the silence linger for a beat too long, as if deciding whether to be intrigued or dismissive.

Finally, he spoke, his voice low, smooth, and full of amusement. "Well, it's not every day I get the chance to meet someone who isn't just another face in the crowd."

Jasmine's lips curled into a smile. Not just another face, she thought, her eyes narrowing slightly as she leaned in just a little closer.

"Do I really look like just another face to you?" she asked, her voice low and inviting.

His smile widened, amused, but something in his expression told her he was intrigued, drawn in by the challenge she presented. He leaned back slightly, appraising her with a look that made her feel like she was being seen—really seen—for the first time in a long time.

"I don't know," he said, his voice dropping an octave. "You're definitely not what I expected."

Jasmine raised an eyebrow, the words almost a challenge of their own. "Then you haven't figured me out yet," she whispered to herself, but aloud, she let her voice remain steady, confident. "Trust me, there's a lot more to me than meets the eye."

He held her gaze, silent for a beat. She felt the pressure building, the quiet exchange of power in the space between them. There was no hesitation in her—she was here for one reason, and that reason was to win.

His eyes lingered on her, sizing her up, and for the first time, Jasmine wondered if maybe he was as intrigued as she was. But he wasn't the type of man who would be impressed easily, and Jasmine knew that was exactly why she was drawn to him.

Chapter 6

"I don't think I've ever met someone like you before," he said finally, his voice teasing, amused, but there was an edge to it. "And I'm not used to being kept on my toes."

Jasmine's pulse quickened at his words, but her smile never wavered. This is what I want. This is the game I want to play, she thought, as her lips parted in a sly grin.

"Well," she said, her voice still playful, but with a tinge of challenge, "I'm full of surprises. But I'd like to think I can keep you entertained."

He stepped in closer, their proximity barely a breath apart, and Jasmine could feel the heat of his body, the magnetic pull between them.

"I'll take you up on that," he said, his tone lowering, his smile turning into something darker, more tempting. "But we'll see if you're as good as you claim."

Jasmine felt the shift—the chemistry, the power, the unspoken understanding that this was a game they were both willing to play. And she was going to win. This was her moment, her time to prove that she was more than just a pretty face in the crowd.

The music continued to pound in the background, but it was as though the world had narrowed to just the two of them, the space between them crackling with an electric energy that neither of them could deny.

Jasmine didn't need to say anything more. The look in his eyes, the subtle challenge in his smile—everything between them had already been said. This was just the beginning, and Jasmine had every intention of playing it out on her terms.

Jasmine couldn't help but smirk to herself as she scanned the party. The atmosphere was electric, with the loud thumping of the bass vibrating through her chest, the flashes of neon lights casting playful glows across the crowd. The air was thick with laughter, conversation, and the smell of expensive cologne and perfume. Everywhere she turned, there were people dancing, chatting, and clinking glasses, all caught up in the rhythm of the night.

She and Sarah walked through the bustling room, their eyes glancing over the scene, taking in the lavish decorations, the plush couches, and the groups gathered around the bar. Jasmine could feel the stares as they passed, the murmurs and whispers of admiration trailing behind them like an invisible curtain.

Sarah leaned in close to Jasmine, her voice hushed but playful, a mischievous grin spreading across her face.

"Sure you want to do this?" Sarah whispered, glancing at the group of people surrounding the tall man she had noticed earlier. "Looks like he's already got a crowd."

Jasmine barely even heard Sarah's words. Her eyes were locked on him. She straightened, her posture sharp as she gave a subtle nod.

"I didn't come here to watch from the sidelines," she muttered softly to herself, the determination in her voice unmistakable.

The crowd seemed to part as she walked through it, each step purposeful, her hips swaying with effortless grace. Her dress, a bold choice for a night like this, caught the light just right, glimmering as she moved. The music, the chatter, the laughter—it all seemed to fade into the background, leaving her in a bubble of focused energy. She was no longer just a face in the crowd; she was the center of attention, and she knew it.

The tall man, casually laughing with his friends, turned his head just as she approached, his gaze meeting hers for a split second. It was electric. The connection was immediate, almost as if he had been waiting for her, sensing her presence from across the room.

Jasmine smiled to herself, feeling the rush of confidence course through her veins. She adjusted the strap of her dress with a flick of her wrist, making sure everything was perfect. She wasn't just going to walk up to him; she was going to make an entrance.

Sarah, a few steps behind, chuckled under her breath, her eyes glinting with amusement and curiosity. Jasmine, however, didn't even glance back. She was locked on him, and the space between them seemed to close with every step she took.

As she neared him, she could feel the heat rising in her chest. She stood tall, her presence undeniable, and her eyes never leaving his. It was now or never. She wasn't going to waste this chance.

With a small but confident smile, she spoke, her voice low and teasing, carrying just the right amount of challenge.

"I thought I'd finally get a chance to meet you," she said, her words dripping with self-assuredness. "I've been watching you all night."

The moment seemed to stretch out, the world around them blurring into insignificance. He paused, clearly surprised by her boldness, but intrigued nonetheless. His gaze softened, and he set his drink down, leaning in slightly as though to catch every word she said.

Jasmine held his stare, her confidence only growing. This was the moment she had been waiting for.

"I've seen a lot of people here tonight, but you—well, you stand out," she added, letting the words hang between them, charged with meaning.

His lips curled into a small smile, a knowing look flashing in his eyes. She could feel him sizing her up, taking her in. It was a silent exchange, a subtle game of cat and mouse, and Jasmine was winning.

"I'm not used to being noticed," he said, his voice smooth, his tone just the right mix of flattered and amused. "But you... you're hard to miss."

Jasmine stepped a little closer, feeling the electricity between them intensify. She could smell the faint scent of his cologne, a rich, musky fragrance that seemed to wrap around her like a promise. Her heart beat a little faster as their proximity grew, but she stood her ground, never once breaking eye contact.

"Well, I'm not the type to blend into the crowd," she replied, her voice soft but full of intent. "I'm sure you can appreciate that."

He nodded slowly, as if acknowledging her confidence, a smile still tugging at his lips. He seemed more intrigued by her with each passing second.

"I think I'm starting to see that," he said, his voice a little deeper now, the words carrying a certain weight. "And I have to admit, I like it."

Jasmine allowed the smile on her lips to widen, her eyes sparkling with a mix of excitement and challenge. She knew she had him right where she wanted him.

"Well," she said, her voice low and playful, "I've got a lot more where that came from."

His eyes flickered with interest, and he leaned in just a little closer, his lips curling into a smile.

"Is that so?" he asked, his tone teasing, yet with a hint of seriousness.

Jasmine nodded, her confidence unwavering. She stepped even closer now, just enough to feel the warmth of his presence, and let the words hang in the air between them.

"You'll just have to stick around to find out," she whispered, her voice soft but edged with promise.

For a moment, neither of them spoke. The party raged on around them, but in this small bubble they had created, time seemed to stretch, the world narrowing to just the two of them. Jasmine could feel the chemistry building, a magnetic pull between them that neither of them could deny.

As they stood there, locked in their silent dance of attraction, Jasmine knew one thing for certain: this was only the beginning.

Jasmine's eyes were still locked on Trey, but her moment of quiet focus was broken when a girl, clearly in a rush, stumbled into them, her drink sloshing out of her cup in an explosion of liquid. The splash hit Jasmine's dress first, then Sarah's, and finally, the girl herself was covered in the mess.

"OH NO!" The girl shrieked, her voice high-pitched and frantic. "My dress! I spent my life savings on this!"

She looked absolutely horrified, as if the world were coming to an end. Her hands shook as she tried to dab at the splashes with the tissue she pulled from her purse, but the damage was already done. Jasmine and Sarah exchanged quick glances, then looked down at their own dresses, both now stained with the same drink. The sight was almost comical, considering how carefully they'd picked their outfits for the evening.

Jasmine's lips twitched into a smile as Sarah couldn't hold it back anymore. Sarah let out a snicker, her eyes flashing with amusement.

"Life savings?" Sarah repeated, barely able to keep the disbelief out of her voice. "On that?" She gestured to the girl's dress, which, despite being obviously expensive, was gaudy and in poor taste.

Jasmine's eyes sparkled with a mischievous glint, and she let out a small laugh, shaking her head. "I mean, if you spent your entire life savings on that, you might want to re-evaluate your spending habits," she said, her voice dripping with sarcasm.

The girl's face flushed with embarrassment, and she tried to swipe at the mess again, only making things worse. Her eyes flickered between Jasmine and Sarah, clearly realizing the two of them were not the most sympathetic audience.

"I'm so sorry, I didn't mean to—" the girl started to babble, her words tumbling out in a rush.

Jasmine lifted one eyebrow, smirking. "It's okay, it's not like we planned on wearing these dresses for long anyway," she said, trying her best to sound nonchalant despite the annoyance she could feel creeping up on her. The truth was, she wasn't thrilled about the stains, but at least they weren't on a dress she had poured her life savings into.

The girl's face turned an even darker shade of red, and she stammered out an apology, continuing to rub at the fabric, but she was so flustered that she didn't even seem to realize she was only making things worse.

Sarah gave Jasmine a playful nudge. "Let's just leave her to it," she said under her breath, her tone light and teasing. "No need to ruin the rest of our night."

Jasmine's smirk deepens as she takes a step closer to the girl, who is still frantically wiping at her dress, now hopelessly smearing the stains further into the fabric.

"Girl," Jasmine says, her voice dripping with sarcasm, "if you're spending your life savings on cheap knock-offs, you've got bigger problems."

The words hit like a slap, and the girl's face falls. Her eyes well up with tears, humiliation washing over her as she realizes she's the joke of the party. She tries to hold it together, but the sting of Jasmine's words is too much. Her lip quivers, and before she can say anything, the tears begin to fall freely down her cheeks.

Sarah, standing beside Jasmine, can't help but put on a dramatic, mock-sympathetic pout. "Aww, don't cry," she says, her voice overly sweet and mocking. "Maybe next time, save up for something that doesn't fall apart at a party."

The taunting tone sends a ripple of laughter through Jasmine and Sarah. The girl stands there, too mortified to speak, as they exchange amused glances.

"You should've known better than to wear something so flimsy," Jasmine adds with a shrug, stepping away from the girl like she's nothing more than a distant memory. She turns back to Sarah, her eyes gleaming with a cruel, satisfied amusement.

The girl stands frozen for a moment, stunned and crushed under the weight of their insults. Her sobs echo through the room as she spins on her heels, running off toward the bathroom, her tears leaving a trail of misery in her wake. The music, the laughter, the sounds of the party—none of it seems to register for her as she disappears into the crowd.

Jasmine and Sarah, however, walk on without a second thought. They slip past the rest of the crowd, their heads held high, the glittering excitement of the party pulsing around them.

"Can you believe that?" Jasmine mutters, shaking her head in disbelief. "What a joke."

Sarah giggles, her voice light with amusement. "Some people just don't get it, do they?"

They share a look, their laughter bubbling up once more. It's moments like this—when they get to tear someone down and walk away unscathed—that make everything feel a little bit sweeter. The air seems to hum with energy as they push forward into the heart of the party, their confidence now almost palpable, as if they own the space.

Neither of them looks back, their thoughts already moving on to more important matters—like the real reason they came to the party. And right now, it was still standing across the room, waiting for Jasmine to make her move.

Jasmine nodded with a smirk, giving the girl one last glance as they walked away. "Best of luck with that," she said, not even bothering to look back as she and Sarah made their way through the crowd, the laughter still bubbling in her chest.

The night was still young, and she had much more important things to focus on than some girl who couldn't hold her drink—or her dignity.

As Jasmine and Sarah moved deeper into the party, the music thumped in her ears, the buzz of conversation rising around them again. Jasmine's gaze flickered back to Trey, and her determination returned in full force. He was still there, talking and laughing with his friends, and she wasn't going to let a little distraction stop her from making her move. The crowd parted for them, and she straightened, ready to continue what she'd started.

Jasmine and her friend walk confidently up to the entrance, their heels clicking against the polished floor, their dresses hugging their figures, perfectly designed to draw attention. The atmosphere shifts as they move toward the velvet rope, ready to enter the exclusive area of the party.

Just as they approach, one of the security guards steps forward, his body blocking their path. He looks them over, his expression serious, and his voice stern.

"Sorry, ladies. This area is reserved for important guests only."

Jasmine's eyes narrow slightly at the unexpected roadblock, but she quickly recovers, not letting the guard's tone rattle her. She's used to getting what she wants, and she's not about to back down now.

Her friend looks at the guard, then at Jasmine, her tone laced with mock surprise. "Important guests? What, are we not good enough for the VIP section now?"

Jasmine smirks, leaning closer to her friend. "Oh, I think we qualify. We are the important guests tonight."

She straightens her back, meeting the guard's gaze with unwavering confidence, letting her words hang in the air as if daring him to question her. There's a brief flicker of hesitation in his eyes, but he doesn't say anything, still standing his ground.

Her friend, with a laugh that borders on condescending, adds, "Isn't it funny how the most 'important' people are always the hardest to spot?"

Jasmine's eyes flicker to the guard, then back to her friend. She knows exactly how to handle this. With a flick of her wrist, she takes a step forward, closer to the velvet rope.

"I'm sure the host wouldn't want to miss the opportunity to meet two women who clearly know how to bring life to a party, don't you think?"

Jasmine immediately bristles at the comment, her eyes narrowing as she steps closer to the security guard. The sharpness in her tone is unmistakable as she delivers her retort, her posture exuding authority.

"Do I look like a commoner to you?" she demands, her voice laced with attitude.

The guard stumbles back slightly, clearly thrown off by the force of her response. His eyes widen as he tries to gather himself, not expecting the confrontation.

"No, no, ma'am. That's not what I meant... it's just that this part of the party is for VIPs," he stammers, fumbling with his words.

Jasmine crosses her arms over her chest, her gaze unflinching as she regards him with a cool, calculated stare.

"And what exactly makes you think we're not VIPs?" she challenges, her voice firm but smooth, as if daring him to offer another objection.

Sarah, standing beside her, casually pulls out her phone with exaggerated motions, acting as if she's unfazed by the situation. She taps a few buttons on the screen, drawing attention to the fact that she's doing anything but what the guard might expect.

"Let me just call my friend real quick—the one who personally invited us," Sarah says, her voice dripping with mock concern.

She holds the phone up to her ear, and although it's obvious to anyone watching that she's scrolling through her social media feed rather than dialing anyone, she plays the part flawlessly.

"Hey, babe! Yeah, we're at the door. You might wanna let these guys know we're with you," she continues, her tone casual but tinged with the kind of superiority that comes from being in on the joke.

The security guard hesitates, clearly unsure of how to handle the situation. His eyes flicker nervously between Jasmine and Sarah, the tension hanging in the air. Just as it seems like the confrontation might escalate, the party host, who has been watching the scene unfold, steps forward with a confident gesture. He raises a hand toward the security team, signaling them to approach.

Chapter 7

One of the guards moves quickly, whispering something into the ear of the first guard. The first guard listens intently, his expression shifting from uncertainty to realization. After a brief moment, he nods stiffly, his posture relaxing a bit.

"Alright, ladies, you're good to go. Enjoy the party," the security guard says, his voice now much less authoritative, almost apologetic.

Jasmine's lips curl into a small, satisfied smirk as she watches the guard back off. She doesn't waste a second, rolling her eyes and pushing past him with an air of superiority. Sarah follows closely behind, both of them striding confidently into the heart of the party.

As they walk away, Jasmine mutters under her breath, her tone laced with a sense of victory. "That's more like it."

The words are barely audible over the hum of the crowd, but the message is clear—Jasmine has won this round, and she knows it. Her eyes scan the room as she moves forward, her confidence palpable, and Sarah is right beside her, equally unbothered by the brief confrontation.

The party's energy intensifies as they enter, but Jasmine's mind is already focused on the next goal: making her presence known and commanding attention.

Jasmine stifles a grin, watching the guard's face turn a shade of pink as he realizes they're not just two girls with a grudge. They're playing the game and winning it. The guard glances between the two of them, clearly unsure how to respond, his previous confidence slipping away.

Jasmine allows a brief pause to hang in the air before she offers him a small, mocking smile. "You should've known better. Now, if you'll excuse us…"

She steps forward, her heels clicking sharply on the floor as she moves past him, Sarah trailing closely behind. As they make their way into the VIP area, Jasmine's smile widens, her victory sweet.

Sarah, ever the one for theatrics, waves her phone in the air one last time before slipping it back into her bag. "It's all about who you know," she says with a wink, as they both glide through the velvet ropes without a second glance at the guard.

Jasmine's eyes flicker across the room, scanning the crowd. She can already feel the eyes on her, and she loves it. This is where she's meant to be. The energy, the people—everything about this moment screams success, and it's only just begun.

The main area of the house party is abuzz with energy. The ambient lighting casts a soft glow over the lavish décor, while the air is thick with the scent of expensive colognes and the rich mix of perfumes. Tables are elegantly arranged with high-end snacks—

glistening platters of sushi, bite-sized hors d'oeuvres, and luxurious chocolate truffles. Servers, dressed in sharp uniforms, move smoothly through the crowd, balancing trays of drinks and appetizers that are sure to impress any guest lucky enough to partake.

Jasmine and Sarah slip into the area effortlessly, their eyes scanning the room, their presence immediately felt. They gravitate toward a table near the center of the action, strategically choosing seats that keep them within clear sight of Trey and his group. Jasmine's eyes flicker toward him every few seconds, her gaze lingering as she silently assesses the scene. Her movements are graceful, deliberate, and confident—she knows exactly how to position herself in a room full of people.

Sarah, still basking in the aftermath of their little victory at the door, throws a smug look at the servers who pass by, their trays heavy with drinks and snacks. Her smile is wide, almost giddy as she whispers to Jasmine, her voice playful.

"See? VIP treatment already," she giggles, nodding toward the servers who are now bringing them drinks. The attention is certainly not lost on her.

Jasmine, however, doesn't immediately respond, her focus shifting slightly as her eyes fall back on Trey. She studies him for a moment, her expression shifting into something more contemplative. It's clear that while she's relishing the attention and luxury around her, her mind is still on him—he's the prize tonight.

Though her lips don't curve into the same smirk as Sarah's, Jasmine can't suppress the slight glimmer of satisfaction in her eyes as she sips her drink. She knows that in this world, power isn't just about wealth or status—it's about getting the right people to notice you. And tonight, that's exactly what she's doing.

With a casual glance, Jasmine notices that Trey is laughing with his friends, looking completely at ease in the crowd. He hasn't noticed her yet, but she's confident that it won't be long before he does. The evening, she thinks, is just beginning.

Jasmine leans back in her chair, swirling her drink as she shoots a pointed glance at Sarah, her lips curling in mild annoyance. Her fingers tap against the glass, a soft rhythm that betrays her impatience. The noise of the party swirls around them, but Jasmine's focus sharpens on the conversation at hand.

"Who invited you to this anyway?" she asks, her voice laced with curiosity and a hint of irritation.

Sarah, who's been half-focused on Trey and his group across the room, barely glances at Jasmine as she shrugs nonchalantly. "My friend..." she trails off, her tone light, but there's an obvious shift in her attention, her gaze flicking back toward Trey with increasing enthusiasm.

Jasmine's eyes narrow slightly. "Which of them?" she presses, not letting the matter slide so easily. She's never one to leave a question unanswered, especially not when it comes to people in Sarah's circle.

"You don't know him," Sarah responds, waving her off with a casual flick of her hand. There's a playful gleam in her eyes, but it's clear that she's more interested in the man across the room than answering Jasmine's question.

"I know all your friends," Jasmine mutters, her irritation bubbling to the surface. She leans in slightly, her voice tinged with challenge. She's not one to be kept in the dark, especially when it involves a party like this, where knowing the right people is half the battle.

Sarah glances at her, a mischievous grin tugging at the corners of her mouth. "Trust me, you don't know this one," she says with a wink, clearly enjoying the mystery.

Jasmine's expression darkens, her annoyance growing as she sits up straighter in her chair. "You know I hate not knowing people at these things," she says, her words cutting through the hum of the party. "I should've been invited first-hand."

Sarah's smile falters just for a second as she realizes Jasmine is genuinely bothered, but then she waves it off with a casual flick of her hand, not at all concerned by Jasmine's frustration.

"Relax," Sarah says, flashing a playful grin. "It doesn't matter. It's just a party."

But Jasmine doesn't seem convinced. As Sarah continues to pretend to be nonchalant, her eyes darting toward Trey again, Jasmine's gaze remains sharp, focused on the situation at hand. She takes a slow sip from her drink, trying to shake off the slight irritation, but deep down, she knows she doesn't like feeling excluded—especially when she's at the top of her game.

And tonight, she intends to stay there.

Jasmine rolls her eyes discreetly as Sarah practically lounges in her seat, throwing flirtatious glances toward Trey. Jasmine feels a wave of irritation creep in again, though she tries to mask it with a casual sip from her drink. The constant pulse of the music reverberates through the floor, mixing with laughter and chatter as the party swirls around them.

Sarah leans back in her chair, flipping her hair with exaggerated flair, her voice light and carefree. "Relax, Jazz! Besides, we're here now, aren't we?" she giggles, obviously excited about the situation, completely unaware of the tension simmering underneath Jasmine's cool exterior.

Jasmine leans back in her chair, swallowing hard, the taste of the drink not quite masking the sourness in her mood. She glances down at her phone, her frustration mounting as she sees several missed calls from her mother, the notifications blurring together. She taps the screen, briefly considering calling her back, but ultimately decides against it. Her mother always seems to find a way to disrupt her fun, and tonight, Jasmine has other things on her mind.

As the two settle into their seats, the crowd around them becomes a blur of movement. The servers move swiftly between tables, balancing trays of drinks and plates of snacks, their footsteps lost in the overwhelming noise of the party. A server arrives at their table, placing a fresh round of drinks in front of them. Jasmine glances at the glasses, her fingers absentmindedly tracing the rim of her own, trying to drown out the persistent thoughts about her mother and the missed calls.

Sarah's voice cuts through her reverie. "I swear, Jazz, this is the best spot in the house. Right next to Trey!" Sarah says, practically vibrating with excitement, her tone a mix of pride and eagerness. She leans forward, arching her back just enough to make sure she catches Trey's eye, her movements bold and deliberate. Jasmine watches, unimpressed.

"Yeah, perfect spot," Jasmine mutters under her breath, her tone laced with a hint of sarcasm, but she keeps her expression neutral. She adjusts herself slightly, sitting up straighter as she takes another slow sip of her drink. Her eyes flicker toward Trey, but only for a moment. She's careful not to seem too eager, but a part of her can't help but feel a surge of satisfaction at being so close to him, despite her annoyance with Sarah's antics.

The party around them continues to buzz, but for Jasmine, the distance between herself and Trey feels palpable. She wants to make her move, but she needs to do it on her terms. She's not going to rush this. Not when she has everything under control.

Jasmine feels a flutter of excitement mixed with an undercurrent of tension as she catches Trey's gaze again. This time, it feels different. There's a moment of quiet recognition between them, an invisible thread pulling them together even though they're still a distance apart. Her pulse quickens, but she does her best to stay composed, her eyes flickering away from his once the connection becomes too intense. She takes another sip of her drink, trying to hide the small smile tugging at her lips.

Sarah, oblivious to the subtle interaction between Jasmine and Trey, continues to giggle uncontrollably, her voice loud and attention-grabbing. "Do you think he's noticed me yet?" she asks, her tone filled with excitement, her eyes scanning the room as if expecting an immediate response.

Jasmine glances at Sarah, forcing herself to look disinterested, but her eyes can't help but flick back to Trey. As if on cue, his gaze flickers toward her again, this time holding her attention for a few moments longer. There's an undeniable spark in the air, and it's as if the room has quieted just for that brief, lingering moment between their eyes.

Jasmine's heart skips a beat, and she finds herself holding her breath for just a fraction of a second. She swallows, her throat dry, and turns her focus back to her drink, hiding the slight flush creeping up her neck. She mutters, her voice low and controlled, "Yeah... something like that."

Sarah, hearing only what she wants to hear, squeals with excitement, leaning in closer to Jasmine. "He totally has! I bet he's thinking about coming over right now!" she says, her voice a mix of giddy anticipation and a touch of teasing. She bounces in her seat, clearly imagining the next steps of her plan unfolding perfectly.

Jasmine doesn't respond immediately, her mind racing. She can feel Sarah's excitement radiating off her, but Jasmine's attention is still on Trey, her thoughts clouded with a mixture of desire and calculation. She's not one to jump at the first opportunity; she wants to make sure this moment—this connection—is hers to control.

Jasmine tries to steady her breath, her fingers gripping her phone a little tighter as she scrolls aimlessly. Every so often, her eyes flick up, almost involuntarily, to steal another glance at Trey. She feels his gaze on her, the weight of it sending a shiver down her spine. It's subtle, but undeniably there—an electric tension that lingers in the air, wrapping itself around her like a pulse she can't escape.

She looks away quickly each time, pretending to be absorbed in her phone, but her heart is pounding faster with every silent moment that stretches between them. There's a kind of thrill in the way he watches her from across the room, leaning back in his chair, his expression relaxed yet filled with a quiet confidence that sends a rush of heat through her.

A small, knowing smile plays at the corners of his lips, and Jasmine can't help but feel a mix of satisfaction and uncertainty. There's something magnetic about him, something that pulls her in without her permission.

She forces herself to keep her focus on the screen, trying to distract herself from the pull of his presence. But inside, she's aware of every movement he makes. The way he leans back just a little further, the subtle tilt of his head as he watches her, the way his eyes never fully leave her. It's like a silent conversation between them, one that speaks louder than any words could.

Her pulse is racing, and yet she refuses to let him see it. Jasmine isn't one to be easily swayed. She'll play this game, but she'll be the one to set the pace.

Jasmine's breath catches in her throat, her heart racing as she holds his gaze. She quickly looks away, trying to mask the sudden flush rising to her cheeks. The intensity of the moment lingers, like an electric charge between them, impossible to ignore. Her fingers fumble with her drink, her usual composure slipping as the space between them seems to shrink.

She's aware of Sarah's voice, still animated and bubbly beside her, but it feels like background noise now. All her attention is consumed by the weight of Trey's gaze on her. She can feel him watching, studying her, and she can't help but wonder what he's thinking. What does he see when he looks at her?

She chides herself for even caring. She doesn't need validation from him. She's not here to impress anyone, certainly not some guy from the other side of the room. But the way he looks at her… it makes her second-guess that resolve.

Trey shifts in his chair, adjusting his posture slightly, but his eyes never leave her. He takes a slow sip from his drink, a small, unreadable smile playing on his lips. It's the kind of smile that makes her wonder if he's amused by the game or if he's about to make his move.

Jasmine forces herself to take a steady breath and straighten her shoulders. She's not going to make this easy. If he wants her attention, he's going to have to earn it.

The music thunders around the room, pulsating through the walls, vibrating the floor beneath their feet. The laughter of the crowd, the clinking of glasses, and the sharp voices of conversation blend into a dizzying cacophony. Jasmine sips her drink, feeling the cool liquid slide down her throat as she watches the party unfold. The room is filled with high-end snacks, glittering chandeliers hanging from the ceiling, their soft, ambient light casting a seductive glow over everything.

She can feel the warmth of the room on her skin, the slight buzz from her drink, but none of it compares to the rush she feels in her chest when she catches a glimpse of him across the room.

She shifts in her seat, her eyes narrowing, as her gaze locks onto him. He's sitting with his friends, his tall frame relaxed in the chair, a confident smile playing at the edges of his lips. His eyes flicker over the crowd, and for a brief second, their gazes meet.

Her heart skips a beat. She quickly looks away, feigning disinterest, but her mind races. She forces herself to act casual, checking her phone to see the screen light up with missed notifications. But in the back of her mind, she's acutely aware of his presence. Even without looking directly at him, she can feel his gaze on her—it's electric.

She takes a slow sip of her drink, pretending to scroll through her phone, but she can't stop herself from glancing up again. There's a pull, a magnetic force between them, as if the air around them has thickened.

As she sneaks another glance, she notices his eyes are still on her. He's looking at her, really looking. The thought sends a wave of heat through her, making her cheeks flush, and a tiny smirk tugs at the corners of her lips. But she quickly suppresses it, keeping her face cool and composed.

She watches as he leans back in his chair, eyes never straying far from her. There's something in his gaze, something that's both confident and curious. She can't quite put her finger on it, but it makes her pulse race.

And then she hears the voice beside her.

"Do you think he's noticed me yet?" The words are full of excitement, oblivious to the fact that the connection between Jasmine and him is palpable, undeniable.

Jasmine raises an eyebrow, trying to hide the small smirk that plays at the edges of her mouth. She's well aware of where his attention lies. "Oh, yeah," she says, her voice smooth, cool. "Totally."

But even as she says it, her mind is elsewhere. She's fighting the urge to look over at him again, to confirm the unspoken tension that's growing between them. She feels the weight of his gaze even when she's not looking, and it sends a shiver down her spine.

Her friend leans in closer, her voice rising in pitch with excitement. "He totally has! I bet he's thinking about coming over right now!"

Chapter 8

Jasmine smiles but doesn't say anything. Her fingers tighten around her glass, the ice cubes clicking together. She's trying to stay composed, trying to not let the flood of emotions—curiosity, excitement, and a hint of frustration—overwhelm her. Sarah is bouncing with excitement, her energy impossible to ignore, but Jasmine can't help feeling a surge of satisfaction. She knows the truth, and it makes her stomach flutter. Trey isn't looking at Sarah the way he's looking at her.

Her friend is so wrapped up in her own world, completely unaware of the silent electricity between Jasmine and Trey. She keeps talking, keeps giggling, as if the entire party revolves around her. Jasmine forces herself to smile, nodding along to Sarah's chatter, all the while trying to suppress the overwhelming surge of thoughts in her mind.

Every time she looks over at him, he's still watching her. It's like he knows she's doing the same, and a silent game begins to unfold between them—one where neither is willing to back down.

The moment feels surreal, like they're the only two people in the room. Jasmine can hear Sarah laughing, hear the clinking of glasses, but all of that fades into the background as she locks eyes with him once more. She can't stop the thrill that courses through her veins, and for the briefest moment, everything feels possible. Everything feels right.

Then Sarah's voice pulls her back to reality.

"I swear, Jazz, this is the best spot in the house," Sarah says, flipping her hair over her shoulder, completely oblivious to the undercurrent of tension between Jasmine and Trey. "Right next to him! I mean, do you see how he's been looking at me? Totally into it."

Jasmine can feel a slight twitch of irritation at the edge of her thoughts. She knows Sarah doesn't mean any harm, but it's hard to ignore the truth—that Trey's attention has been on her, not on Sarah.

"Yeah," Jasmine says, her voice carefully neutral. "Perfect spot."

She says it without a hint of emotion, trying to make it sound casual, but inside, she's seething. How long can she play this game? How long can she pretend that she doesn't feel the pull between them?

Just then, she feels his gaze again, more intense than ever. He's looking at her with such focus that it almost feels like he's standing right in front of her, but he's still across the room. The connection is undeniable.

Jasmine forces herself to look away, focusing on the drink in her hand, but she can't stop the grin that spreads across her face.

It's like he's daring her to do something, anything, to acknowledge this magnetic pull between them.

Sarah is still gushing about how Trey is probably thinking of coming over to talk to her, but Jasmine knows the truth. She can feel it, deep in her bones—Trey is thinking about her.

Her phone vibrates in her hand, a distraction, but it's only one more missed call from her mother. Jasmine ignores it, her mind focused solely on the moment unfolding before her. She takes a deep breath and glances back over at Trey. He's still watching her, still looking at her with that same intensity.

Jasmine's heart races in her chest. There's a part of her that wants to turn away, to make him work for her attention, but another part—an undeniably strong part—wants to lean into this. She can feel the challenge in his eyes. And she's ready to accept it.

"Do you think he's coming over?" Sarah asks again, her voice filled with expectation.

Jasmine lets out a breath, finally letting her composure slip just slightly as she tilts her head toward Sarah. "Maybe," she murmurs, a knowing smile curling at her lips.

This isn't over. Not by a long shot.

Jasmine said with a smile, "Let's see how this goes."

The music dims, and the atmosphere shifts as the host grabs the mic, commanding the crowd's attention. The energy in the room changes immediately, everyone growing quieter in anticipation.

The host said aloud, with enthusiasm. "Alright, y'all! It's time! Make some noise for Trey!"

The crowd erupts into applause and cheers, excitement buzzing through the air as Trey steps confidently onto the stage, mic in hand. Jasmine's eyes widen in surprise, and she leans toward her friend.

Jasmine said, surprised, "Trey's a rapper?"

Her friend, practically bursting with excitement, beams, her eyes dancing as she responds.

Her friend said, grinning widely, "Girl, I didn't know either! This just makes him perfect!"

Jasmine can't help but smile softly, her curiosity piqued. She watches as Trey, now on stage, adjusts the mic and raises his hand to signal for the crowd to settle down. His demeanor is effortless, commanding the room with a cool, composed presence. As the crowd quiets, Jasmine feels a rush of intrigue—there's something magnetic about him. She can't tear her eyes away as he readies himself to perform.

Trey said, with a grin, "Alright, alright. Let's turn this up, huh?"

The crowd cheers, and the DJ kicks in with the music, the bass dropping and the rhythm quickening. Trey begins to rap, and his body moves fluidly with the music. The crowd hangs on every word, and Jasmine feels an electric charge in the air as she watches him perform. It's smooth, precise, and incredibly captivating. She finds herself drawn deeper into his performance, her attention fixed solely on him.

Her friend said, loudly over the music, "Did you hear that? He's so good! I bet he's gonna blow up after this. He's got that flow!"

Jasmine nods absently, her eyes still locked on him. There's something about his energy, the way he moves, the way he owns the stage—it's magnetic. Her heart skips a beat as Trey's eyes briefly scan the crowd and land on her. She's caught in the intensity of that moment, a brief connection that leaves her breathless.

Her friend, still in awe, keeps cheering, not noticing the shift in Jasmine's demeanor as she becomes more entranced by Trey's performance. Jasmine's mind races, and a part of her wonders if there's something more to that fleeting glance.

As Trey finishes his verse, the crowd erupts into applause, and he steps back, grinning as he signals the DJ to drop the next track. The music shifts again, but the energy remains, the afterglow of his performance still pulsing through the room. Jasmine feels the beat resonate in her chest, her thoughts lingering on him, unsure of how to process what just happened.

She exhales slowly, letting the moment wash over her. There's no denying it—there's something about him that she can't ignore.

On stage, Trey starts his performance, effortlessly flowing through a smooth melody with a rap edge. His voice commands the room, cutting through the bass-heavy beats with ease. Each lyric rolls off his tongue like it's second nature, and his confidence is undeniable. The crowd responds immediately, hyped by his presence, but Jasmine can't help but focus solely on him.

Her eyes follow his every move as he shifts across the stage, owning every inch of it with a kind of effortless swagger. She crosses her arms, trying to play it cool, but inside, a spark of something she can't quite place flickers. Her heart beats a little faster, matching the rhythm of the music that pulses through the room.

Trey's gaze sweeps over the crowd, and for a split second, their eyes lock. Jasmine feels a jolt run through her, her breath catching in her throat, but she quickly looks away, pretending to focus on the drink in her hand. She tells herself to play it casual—after all, she can't be the one to look too eager.

But she knows, deep down, that she's completely captivated by him, by the way he commands the stage and the crowd. And it isn't just his music—there's something magnetic about him, something that draws her in and makes it impossible to look away.

As Trey continues, the energy in the room intensifies, and Jasmine feels herself getting lost in the rhythm. Every beat, every verse, seems to echo inside her, syncing with the pulse of the party and her racing thoughts. She tries to focus, tries to remind herself that she's here for a reason, but her mind keeps wandering back to him.

Jasmine muttered under her breath, trying to make sense of what was happening. I didn't expect this... Her words were barely audible over the pounding beat of the music, but she couldn't stop her mind from racing. She had come here expecting a night of mindless fun, maybe a few laughs with friends, but this? This was entirely different. She hadn't anticipated feeling like this, so caught up in the heat of the moment, her pulse quickening with every beat of the song.

Sarah, lost in her own world, was practically vibrating with excitement. She leaned closer to Jasmine, her eyes wide with adoration as she watched the performance unfold.

"I think I'm in love! Look at him!" Sarah squealed, her voice high-pitched with admiration. Jasmine glanced at Sarah, but all she could see was the man on stage, his every movement smooth, controlled, and undeniably charismatic.

Jasmine wasn't sure if it was the music, the atmosphere, or the undeniable pull she felt in her chest, but something was changing. She was no longer just a casual observer of the scene; she was in the middle of it, wrapped up in the energy of the crowd, the electric charge between her and him.

Just as Jasmine started to process the whirlwind of emotions that were building inside her, the unexpected happened. Trey, still rapping, jumped off the stage, stepping confidently into the crowd. His presence seemed to part the sea of partygoers as if they were instinctively making space for him. Jasmine's heart skipped a beat, her eyes widening as their gazes locked.

For a moment, the music faded into the background. The crowd seemed to disappear. It was just the two of them, the heat of his stare so intense she could almost feel it against her skin.

Jasmine's breath caught in her throat. Her fingers gripped the edge of the table in front of her, but she couldn't tear her eyes away from him.

He moved effortlessly through the crowd, his eyes never leaving hers, and she felt rooted to the spot, unable to move or speak. Every muscle in her body seemed frozen, but her mind was on fire. What was happening? Why was he walking directly toward her? It was all too surreal, like something out of a dream, but there was no denying that it was happening.

Jasmine's pulse raced as Trey closed the distance between them, and with a sudden shift, he was standing right in front of her. He didn't glance at anyone else around him. His gaze remained fixed solely on her, and the space around them seemed to shrink, the noise and music fading even more as he leaned in, his face inches from hers.

Then, in the most unexpected move of all, he gently licked her cheek. Jasmine's eyes widened, and she gasped, completely caught off guard. Did he just...? The shock of the gesture hit her hard. Her skin tingled where he had touched it, her heartbeat echoing in her ears.

Jasmine's hands trembled slightly, her mind scrambling to process what had just happened. This was not the night she had planned. Not even close. She opened her mouth to say something, to ask him why, but before she could form a coherent thought, he was already moving again.

Trey grinned, the expression in his eyes playful yet intense, as if he had done exactly what he wanted to do and enjoyed every second of it. With a smooth, confident motion, he extended his hand to her. The crowd was still buzzing, but it felt like the two of them existed in a world of their own, completely disconnected from everything around them.

"Come dance with me," he said, his voice low, almost a whisper, but still carrying the weight of his charm.

Jasmine blinked, her mind a whirlwind of thoughts, but before she could respond, he was already pulling her to her feet. His hand was warm in hers, his grip gentle but firm. The touch sent a jolt through her, a strange electricity running up her arm and straight to her chest. She stumbled slightly as he guided her through the crowd, her heart racing, her breath quickening. Every step felt surreal. Her head was spinning, and she couldn't stop herself from glancing around, trying to ground herself in the reality of it all.

Sarah stood frozen in place, watching the scene unfold with wide eyes, completely stunned by what she was witnessing. The change in the air was palpable—what had started as an evening of excitement and flirtation had suddenly become something entirely different. Sarah mumbled to herself, barely audible over the loud music.

"What the hell..." she whispered, her voice filled with disbelief.

Jasmine's mind was a blur as she tried to wrap her head around the fact that she was now being led toward the front of the room, right into the heart of the party. She glanced at Trey, but he was already focused on the rhythm, his body moving with the music. He spun her gently as they reached the center, his hands never leaving her waist. The crowd around them seemed to fade away as the music enveloped them both, a seamless connection between the beat and their movements.

For a moment, everything felt suspended in time. Jasmine was no longer thinking about the world around her, no longer worried about anything except the way her body responded to the beat and the closeness between her and Trey. His touch was magnetic, drawing her closer, making her forget the rest of the world.

Her movements, though a little hesitant at first, became more fluid as she matched his rhythm. She was no longer worried about looking awkward or out of place. There was no room for self-consciousness when everything felt this right. The energy between them was electric, the pull undeniable, and Jasmine couldn't help but lean in just a little bit closer.

As they danced, she found herself drawn deeper into the moment, her mind racing but also somehow at ease. She wasn't sure what had just happened or what was going to happen next, but for the first time in a long time, she felt alive, caught up in the music, the connection, and the sheer thrill of it all.

Every beat of the music seemed to match the rhythm of her heart, and for a moment, she could almost forget that the rest of the world existed. It was just them—Trey, with his infectious confidence and undeniable charisma, and her, caught up in the whirlwind of it all.

The crowd's cheers echo around them, but Jasmine barely hears them, lost in the moment. The energy between her and Trey crackles like static, making everything else feel far away. She's no longer just a spectator in the room; she's part of something—something electric and thrilling.

Trey continues to rap, his words directed straight at her, and it feels like they're the only two people in the world right now. His hand is on her lower back, steadying her as they move together in time with the music. Jasmine's breath comes faster with every beat. The room spins, but it's as if they're in their own bubble. His presence is magnetic, drawing her in deeper with each verse he spits, each line he delivers directly to her.

His gaze holds hers, intense and focused, as if he's the only one who sees her, the only one who matters in this moment. Jasmine's heart races, a mix of surprise and excitement filling her chest. She couldn't have predicted this, not in a thousand years. And yet, here she is, dancing with the guy everyone else is talking about, the guy with a voice that seems to weave through her, the guy who's rapping to her like it's just the two of them.

"What's the name?" Trey asks, his voice low, full of curiosity. It's an effortless question, but the way he says it makes Jasmine feel like she's the most important person in the room.

"Jasmine," she replies, her voice breathless, a small smile tugging at her lips as she keeps her eyes locked on his.

"I didn't know you were this good," she adds, her voice quieter, the compliment slipping out before she can stop it. Her pulse is still racing, but now it's not just from the music. It's the way Trey's eyes are on her—like he's not just performing but connecting, deeply.

Trey smirks, the playful look in his eyes never leaving. "You ain't seen nothing yet," he replies, leaning in just a bit closer. The scent of his cologne surrounds her, mixing with the beat of the music that seems to match the quickening pace of her heart. His lips are mere inches from her ear as he continues.

And then, his voice drops even lower, barely above a whisper, but it's not just for her to hear—it's for her to feel. The words flow from him effortlessly, almost like a spell.

"You're the one I've been searching for... I felt it the moment you walked through that door..."

Jasmine's breath catches in her throat. Every word feels like it's seeping into her, pulling her in further, deeper into the moment. It's not just the lyrics. It's the intensity in his voice, the sincerity that somehow slips through the casual tone of his rap. For a second, she forgets everything—everything but him, his voice, and the way he's looking at her like she's the only thing that matters in this crowded room.

She tries to steady herself, to cling to some sense of reality, but the way Trey moves with her, the way he's holding her, the way he's rapping to her—it's all too much to ignore. She can't resist, can't fight the pull between them.

As they sway together, Jasmine feels a warmth spread through her, the heat of his body just inches from hers. It's intoxicating, and she's caught up in it. He's guiding her, his hands firm but gentle, and the way his body moves to the beat is mesmerizing. He pulls her closer, and for a split second, Jasmine wonders if this is all real or if she's dreaming.

Chapter 9

Her hands move instinctively, finding their place on his shoulders, matching his movements. The music seems to pulse through her veins, and for a moment, it feels like the world is fading away. All that matters is the here and now. His presence, his words, his touch.

And then, Trey smirks again, pulling back just enough to look at her, his eyes scanning her face as if he's savoring the way she reacts to him. There's a spark in his eyes, a glimmer of something playful, but also something much deeper, something that makes Jasmine's breath hitch.

"What do you think?" he asks, his voice teasing now, but there's an edge to it—a hint of something more. "You feelin' this?"

Jasmine pauses, her breath still heavy from the dance and the intensity of the moment. She doesn't know how to answer. She doesn't know if she's ready to admit just how much she's feeling. She's been swept up in it, caught up in the rhythm and the connection between them, but this—this is real, and she's not sure what to do with that.

But before she can say anything, he's leaning in again, and the heat between them is palpable. The crowd fades even further, their cheers and applause distant sounds, as Trey's presence seems to fill her entire world. His lips brush against her ear, and she shivers, unsure if it's from the coolness of the night air or the heat of the moment.

"You don't need to say anything," he murmurs. "Just keep dancing with me. Let the music do the talking."

And so, she does.

Jasmine's smile is soft but full of meaning, as if she's suddenly aware of the delicate weight of the moment. Her heart still races, the rhythm of it syncing perfectly with the last fading notes of the music. She stands there, almost suspended in time, her gaze locked with Trey's. It feels like the world around them has quieted, leaving only the electricity between them, thick and palpable.

Trey, still holding her close, doesn't seem to want to break the connection either. His eyes are searching hers, intense yet tender. His hand rests on her waist, his thumb idly tracing small circles on her skin. Jasmine feels it, the warmth of his touch, the lingering effect of his presence, and she can't help but wonder if he feels it too.

For a moment, there's no need for words. The silence between them is comfortable, almost charged, like an unspoken understanding passing between them. Jasmine, still breathless from the dance, tries to steady herself, but every beat of her heart seems to pulse in time with the way Trey is looking at her. His eyes soften as he leans in slightly, a playful smirk tugging at the corner of his mouth.

"You alright?" Trey asks, his voice low but filled with an undeniable sweetness, as if he's genuinely concerned about her in this intimate moment.

Jasmine takes a deep breath, finally breaking eye contact for a split second. She quickly glances around the room, catching the eyes of a few curious partygoers. But they don't matter right now. Her attention snaps back to Trey, and she nods, her lips curving into a smile that's more genuine than anything she's felt all night.

"I'm fine," she says softly, her voice a little breathless but steady. She can't quite find the right words to express the whirlwind of emotions inside her. So she doesn't try. Instead, she lets the silence linger, feeling the unspoken connection between them.

Trey seems to read her, his eyes scanning her face with a mixture of curiosity and something deeper. A quiet moment stretches between them, thick with possibility. His hand moves from her waist, but only to gently brush a strand of hair away from her face, his fingers lingering just a moment too long on her skin.

"You sure?" His voice is barely a whisper now, but it's all Jasmine can hear.

She nods again, her heart racing for reasons she can't entirely explain. Everything feels so natural yet so intense at the same time, like this is exactly where she's supposed to be, in his presence, at this moment.

"I'm sure," she responds, her voice steadying as she lets out a breath. "I just... wasn't expecting all of this."

The words are out before she can stop them, and it's as if a weight lifts off her chest just by admitting it. She hadn't expected the performance, hadn't expected the way Trey's rapping had wrapped around her like an invisible thread, pulling her closer into this strange, exhilarating world.

Trey chuckles softly, a warm, almost teasing sound that makes her stomach flutter. "I get that a lot." He pauses, his expression softening into something almost more vulnerable. "But you handled it well."

Jasmine smiles, feeling a heat rise to her cheeks. She's never been one to get swept up in things easily, but this—this was different. Trey was different. She didn't know where this was going, or if it was even going anywhere, but she couldn't deny that she was drawn to him in a way she hadn't been with anyone in a long time.

The room starts to fill with chatter again as the music transitions to a different track, but neither of them moves to leave the spot they're standing in. It's like they've created their own little bubble, a space where it's just the two of them, lost in the moment.

"So, Jasmine," Trey says, breaking the silence, his voice playful again, "what do you do when you're not making everyone around you lose their minds with your smile?"

Jasmine laughs softly, the sound light and airy, as if he's somehow managed to disarm her without even trying. "I'm just trying to keep up with the world around me," she replies, her tone teasing, but there's an honesty in it too.

Trey's eyes sparkle with amusement as he takes a step back, but not too far. He's still within arm's reach, his presence undeniable. "I think you're doing a great job," he says, his words a compliment wrapped in that playful tone of his. "But tell me, what else do you like to do? Aside from making random guys like me lose their focus?"

Jasmine raises an eyebrow, her smile widening. "Oh, I've got a lot of tricks up my sleeve. Maybe I'll show you sometime."

His grin grows wider, but there's a genuine curiosity in his eyes now, one that makes Jasmine wonder if this isn't just a flirtation, but something more. She can't quite put her finger on it, but something about the way he's looking at her suggests that he might actually want to know more. Not just about her smile, but about her—who she really is.

Before she can say anything else, Trey gestures toward the crowd, where people are still clapping and dancing. "Well," he says, "if you're not busy, I'm sure we could keep this little dance party going. I could use someone who actually knows how to keep up with me."

Jasmine laughs again, feeling a sense of ease wash over her. This wasn't just some random party encounter. There was something real here, something worth exploring. But whether she was ready to dive into whatever this was… well, that was a question for later.

"Let's see if you can keep up with me, then," she says, her voice playful, but with an underlying challenge. She's still trying to keep her cool, but deep down, she knows this moment is one she won't forget anytime soon.

And as Trey takes her hand once more, leading her back into the crowd, she realizes that whatever happens next, she's not just standing on the sidelines anymore. She's part of something. Part of this.

Jasmine feels the heat rise in her cheeks as she tries to regain her composure, but the smile that tugs at her lips is hard to hide. Trey's words echo in her mind, and for a split second, she wonders if this is really happening. She's still in disbelief—everything about this moment feels like something straight out of her daydreams.

Trey, sensing her momentary pause, chuckles softly, his hand never leaving her waist as he leads her back into the rhythm of the crowd. His touch is confident, sure, but not possessive—just enough to remind her that she's here, with him, in this very moment. The music swirls around them, vibrant and full of energy, but it's as if Jasmine and Trey exist in their own little world.

"You know, you're a lot cooler than I thought you'd be," Trey says, his voice smooth but with a playful edge. He lets go of her waist briefly to twirl her, but his hand quickly finds its way back, resting comfortably on her hip as they continue to move together to the beat.

Jasmine can't help but laugh at the compliment, shaking her head. "You don't know the half of it."

"Maybe I'm starting to," Trey replies, his eyes glinting with amusement. "But I'll need to keep dancing to find out."

Jasmine smirks, not quite sure how to respond to that. She's never been one for flashy compliments or exaggerated gestures, but the way Trey speaks to her—so naturally, like they've known each other for years—it's both flattering and disarming. She feels herself letting go of the doubts and the tension she didn't even realize she was holding onto.

The energy around them shifts slightly, and Jasmine can feel Sarah's gaze from across the room, though she tries to ignore it. She's not sure why, but the mix of jealousy and disbelief in Sarah's expression stirs something inside her. It's not like she was trying to outshine anyone or steal someone else's spotlight, but it's hard not to notice the way Trey has fully centered his attention on her.

"I think you're turning a few heads," Trey says, his voice just loud enough for her to hear over the music. His eyes flicker toward the crowd, where some partygoers have taken notice of their dance. Jasmine feels a subtle flush on her cheeks at the thought, but she's not as concerned about who's watching anymore. For the first time tonight, it's just about the moment—about this.

Jasmine shifts her gaze, catching Sarah's eyes for a brief second. Sarah's face tightens, her lips pursed in what seems like quiet frustration. Jasmine almost feels bad for her friend, but at the same time, she can't deny the exhilaration she feels from Trey's attention. She quickly looks away, not wanting to linger too long on the thought.

The song changes again, the tempo picking up, and Trey grins. "This one's more my style."

He pulls her closer, guiding her through the faster beat with ease. Jasmine follows his lead, the two of them effortlessly in sync. Trey moves with such confidence, his body naturally swaying to the music, while Jasmine mirrors his movements, feeling more alive than she has all night.

The heat between them is undeniable. Their bodies brush in just the right ways, their movements flowing together like a dance they've been practicing for ages. Jasmine can feel the rush of the music coursing through her veins, and she lets herself go completely, not caring about anything else but the beat and the man in front of her.

As the music continues to pulse around them, Trey leans in closer, his lips almost touching her ear as he speaks. "You're not like anyone else here, you know that?"

Jasmine feels a shiver run down her spine at his words. The way he says it—low and intimate—sends an unexpected thrill through her. She's never been the type to fall for the smooth talk, but there's something about Trey that feels different.

She swallows hard, trying to keep her composure. "What do you mean?"

Trey pulls back just enough to look at her, his gaze steady and intense. "You're real. And that's rare. I'm starting to like that about you."

The compliment hangs in the air between them, and Jasmine feels a warmth spread through her chest. She's not used to being seen like this—not the way he sees her. It's not just about how she looks or what she's doing in the moment; it feels like he's actually trying to understand her.

She smiles softly, her heart still racing, but this time for a different reason. "Well, I'm not like everyone else, that's for sure."

Trey grins, clearly enjoying the banter. He twirls her once more before pulling her back into him, his hand now resting gently on her back. "I like that," he murmurs, his voice filled with a certain warmth.

Jasmine's mind is spinning, caught in the whirlwind of the night and the way Trey is looking at her, like she's the only person in the room. Everything else—the crowd, the noise, Sarah's lingering gaze—it all fades into the background as she focuses solely on Trey and the magnetic energy between them. She's not sure where this is going, or if it's even going anywhere, but for right now, she doesn't care. This moment is everything.

As the song winds down, Trey pulls away slightly, but his hand doesn't leave her side. He looks at her with a mixture of admiration and something else—something she can't quite place, but it makes her pulse quicken all over again.

"You're a hell of a dancer, Jasmine," he says, his voice low and appreciative.

Jasmine laughs softly, a little breathless from the dance. "I could say the same about you."

Trey's eyes sparkle with a hint of mischief as he steps closer again, his lips curving into a smirk. "I'm just getting started. You think you can keep up?"

Jasmine meets his challenge with a playful glint in her eyes. "Bring it on."

And with that, they continue to move together, the music wrapping around them like a cocoon, leaving everything else behind. The night has only just begun, and for the first time, Jasmine feels like she's exactly where she's meant to be.

Chapter 10

The dim glow of the lamp casts long shadows across the living room as she paces nervously, phone tightly gripped in her hand. She presses the contact again, listening to the phone ring endlessly. With each passing moment, her anxiety grows.

Her eyes flicker back to the phone as the call goes to voicemail for the third time. She huffs in frustration, pacing faster now, her fingers tapping anxiously on the windowsill. The quiet night outside only deepens her unease.

She presses the number once more, this time holding the phone closer to her ear, as though expecting an answer to materialize from the silence.

"Come on… pick up," she mutters, her voice barely a whisper, as if speaking the words could somehow make them true.

The call rings again, and her worry deepens. Her mind races with scenarios—something must have gone wrong, surely. Why wasn't there any answer?

She stops, glancing at the phone in her hand with growing frustration. With a quick motion, she ends the call and tries again. Each ring is like a hammering beat in her chest. The feeling of helplessness only intensifies, like a weight pressing down on her shoulders.

"What's going on?" she whispers to herself, hoping for some kind of explanation, but there's nothing. The ringing continues, unanswered, and the familiar voice of the voicemail system answers once more.

Her eyes move to the window, where the streetlights cast long shadows over the empty sidewalk. There's an unsettling stillness in the neighborhood, almost too quiet, too empty. She shakes her head as if trying to shake off the growing sense of unease that threatens to consume her thoughts.

After another moment of staring out into the night, she turns, walking briskly toward the door. Her heart races, and her grip on the phone tightens as though somehow, this time, the answer will come. But as she waits, all she hears is the ringing, the cold silence between each tone making her pulse quicken.

She stops and presses the phone back to her ear, calling again, her voice trembling slightly as she leaves a message.

"I'm starting to get really worried. Please just pick up... let me know you're okay."

After she finishes, she ends the call with a shaky hand. The quiet that follows feels deafening. Her heart is in her throat, her thoughts swirling in a haze of worry.

The time is slipping by, too much time—she's been waiting too long. Almost two hours later, the dread turns into a sharp feeling in her chest.

Without another thought, she grabs her coat from the chair by the door and heads out into the night. The chill of the air cuts at her, but it's nothing compared to the cold feeling settling in her stomach. She doesn't stop to think—she can't. The only thing that matters now is finding what's wrong.

She stands there for a moment, eyes closed, her heart heavy with concern. The silence in the room feels overwhelming as she stays in her kneeling position, her hands tightly clasped in prayer.

"Lord, please watch over her tonight," she whispers softly, her voice carrying the weight of every mother's fear and hope. "Keep her safe, wherever she may be."

The words tumble out like a prayer she's said countless times before, but tonight, there's an urgency she can't shake. Each plea feels more desperate than the last.

"I know she's out there... trying to find her way. Help her make the right choices, Lord. Help her find her path back home safely." Her voice cracks slightly, but she continues. "I trust You... I have to trust You."

Her thoughts drift, and she remembers the days when Jasmine was small, running around the house with an energy only youth could bring. Those days felt so long ago, and now, she can't help but feel the distance between them growing with every unanswered ring.

"Please... just let me hear from her. I know she's strong, but Lord, she's still my baby."

A faint shiver runs through her as she slowly rises to her feet. The room feels cold now, the air thick with the unspoken worries of a mother who has lost track of time, waiting for a call that doesn't come. Her gaze lingers on the phone, still untouched on the nightstand, the screen lifeless.

Her heart beats loudly in her chest as she steps back, crossing the room. She hesitates by the window for a moment, watching the world outside—a quiet street, the dark sky, and the soft glow of the streetlights casting long shadows. She stares at nothing in particular, her mind drifting, hoping for an answer, praying for something, anything, to bring her peace.

"Please, Lord," she murmurs again, this time more to herself than to the heavens. "Grant me the strength to bear this."

For a moment, the quiet is all-encompassing. The worries are too much to bear, the unknown too vast to navigate. She finally exhales deeply, closing her eyes briefly as if surrendering to the weight of it all. With one last glance at the phone, she picks it up again, her finger hovering over the call button.

But then she stops. Her grip loosens, and she places the phone back on the nightstand. She knows there's nothing more she can do now but wait, and pray. She doesn't want to give in to the panic that threatens to consume her, but the fear in her heart is undeniable.

Taking another deep breath, she heads back to the window, looking out into the night again. But it feels like a lifetime has passed since the phone call. And yet, no sign of her child. Nothing to tell her that everything will be okay. She says one final prayer, asking for patience, knowing that's the only thing she can hold on to right now.

"I trust You," she whispers, though even she can hear the uncertainty in her own voice. "Please... bring her back to me."

With a soft sigh, Mrs. Thompson finishes her prayer, her hands still clasped together for a moment longer as if unwilling to let go of the fragile hope that it might bring. Slowly, she rises to her feet, the weight of the night pressing down on her. She moves toward her bed, the quiet of the house surrounding her, amplifying the anxiety that churns inside her.

She pulls the blankets over her body, their warmth offering a small sense of comfort, but the peace she longs for feels out of reach. Her eyes, heavy with worry, drift toward the phone once more, still sitting silently on the nightstand. The screen remains dark, offering no answers, no calls, just the endless waiting that has filled the hours.

The room is eerily still, the faint tick of the clock on the wall the only sound breaking the silence. The worries in her heart remain, insistent and unrelenting. Despite the quiet of the night, her mind races with thoughts of Jasmine—where she is, who she's with, and whether she's okay.

She whispers, almost to herself, the words trembling slightly as they leave her lips.

"God, keep her safe tonight."

She rolls over, pulling the blanket closer to her chin, but sleep doesn't come. Not tonight. Her thoughts swirl around Jasmine, wondering what her daughter is doing, whether she's safe, whether she's okay. The unease coils tighter around her chest as every passing second without word from Jasmine feels like an eternity.

She shifts, restless, her eyes flicking back to the phone again. Her mind races through the possibilities—the worst-case scenarios creeping into her thoughts, though she tries to push them aside, holding on to the small thread of hope that Jasmine will come home safe.

The night seems to stretch on endlessly, and no matter how many times she tries to close her eyes, the worry doesn't let her go. It wraps itself around her heart, tightening with every passing moment, making sleep feel impossible. Her mind drifts back to the memory of when Jasmine was young, always so sure of herself, always so eager to find her way. She hopes, prays, that tonight is just another phase, a moment of freedom, a time when Jasmine is out discovering herself, but she can't shake the fear that something might be wrong.

Mrs. Thompson exhales slowly, her body still, but her mind too active to rest. She turns over again, staring into the darkness of the room, her eyes tracing the outlines of the furniture, the shadows cast by the soft glow of the streetlights outside. She doesn't know how long she's been lying there, but the tension in her chest doesn't fade. It lingers, suffocating, as she waits for the sound of her phone ringing, praying that it will be Jasmine on the other end.

But the minutes continue to slip by, one after another, with nothing but silence to answer her worries.

The party atmosphere had started to wind down. The once-thumping beats of the music were now a mere echo in the background, the crowd thinning out as people began to filter out of the venue. Outside, the cool night air mingled with the last flickers of neon lights. The stars above were barely visible, hidden behind the glowing lights of the city, but in that moment, it didn't matter. The world seemed to hold its breath.

The two of them stood near the exit, their voices low and intimate, the intensity of their conversation growing with each passing moment. She felt the electrifying pull of his presence, his words weaving around her like a spell. He stood with such confidence, his eyes never leaving hers, his smile so genuine it made her heart race.

"You're something special," he said, his voice smooth, as though every word was carefully chosen. "I can already see it in you. You've got the star quality, the kind of presence that makes people stop and look. I could see you and me, making real magic together."

Her pulse quickened. She couldn't deny the excitement rising in her chest. The thrill of something unknown, something bigger, something beyond her grasp but right there in front of her, filled her mind.

"What do you mean?" she asked breathlessly, her curiosity piqued by his every word.

His grin widened, a twinkle of mischief in his eyes as he leaned in, lowering his voice just slightly, as if to make their conversation feel even more exclusive.

"I'm talking about a whole new life," he said, his words carrying weight, filled with promise. "Money, fame, everything you could dream of. I want you in my next music video. You could be the face that everyone talks about. We'll turn you into a sensation."

His words hung in the air between them, pulling her in deeper, faster. She couldn't quite comprehend how everything was moving so quickly, yet it felt like the most natural thing in the world. She couldn't stop imagining what it would be like—how different her life could be if she said yes.

He reached into his pocket and pulled out a sleek, black business card. It gleamed under the soft light, and he handed it to her with an air of finality, as though what he was offering was the key to everything.

"Come by my office tomorrow," he continued, his voice full of enthusiasm. "Around 10 AM. We'll go over everything, finalize the deal. You won't regret it."

She took the card from him, her fingers trembling ever so slightly. She felt like she was holding a piece of her future in her hand, a tangible thing that could lead her to somewhere she had only ever dreamed about.

"I'll be there," she said, a bright smile spreading across her face. Her voice was filled with excitement, but there was something deeper there too—a spark of something more, something real. "Thank you. This... this is everything."

He winked at her, his smile playful yet full of promise. "I'm looking forward to it."

With that, he turned and walked toward his car, his confident stride leaving her standing there, breathless and in awe. She watched him disappear into the night, her mind racing as the night's events settled into something solid, something monumental.

Still holding the business card in her hand, she couldn't help but feel like the world had just opened up before her. This was it— her chance to change everything.

Just as she was about to take a moment to collect herself, she heard footsteps approaching from behind. It was her friend, hurrying toward her, her face a mixture of excitement and confusion.

"Girl, what just happened?" her friend asked, practically breathless, a wide grin spreading across her face as she came to stand beside her. "You look like you're floating. What's going on?"

Turning toward her friend, her smile was almost blinding, her eyes sparkling with excitement. The rush of everything that had just happened, the possibility of what was coming, made her feel like she was living in a dream.

"He offered me a chance to be in his next music video," she said, her voice filled with awe. "I'm meeting him tomorrow at his office. This is going to be huge."

Her friend's eyes widened, her mouth falling open in disbelief. "No way! Are you serious? This is everything, girl!"

She nodded, her heart racing as she thought about it again. "I can't believe it either. This could change everything."

Her friend's grin only grew wider. "You've got this, girl. You're going to be amazing."

The two of them shared a laugh, but deep down, she could feel the weight of what was about to happen. This wasn't just a chance—it was the start of something she'd been waiting for, something bigger than she could have ever imagined. She was on the edge of a new life, and nothing would ever be the same again.

As Jasmine and Sarah step away from the venue, Sarah hurries to catch up, her voice full of curiosity but tinged with a hint of concern.

"Hey, Jasmine! What was that all about?" she asks, looking at her friend with a mixture of intrigue and skepticism.

Jasmine turns to her, a sparkle in her eyes betraying the excitement bubbling inside her. But she keeps the details close to her chest, her lips curling into a mysterious smirk.

"Oh, you know… just some business stuff," Jasmine responds casually, but her voice is laced with an excitement she can't completely hide. "I'll fill you in later."

Sarah, ever the one to probe for answers, raises an eyebrow but doesn't press the issue. She's learned when to back off, sensing that Jasmine's not in the mood to share everything just yet.

"Alright, keep your secrets. I'm sure it's going to be amazing!" Sarah teases, her tone playful. She can't help but admire how Jasmine always manages to keep things under wraps, leaving her wondering what exactly went down.

Jasmine nods, still feeling the electric pulse of the night coursing through her veins. She's caught in the afterglow of the performance, the way Trey had looked at her, the opportunity that had just been handed to her. The night felt like a blur, but in the best way possible.

"Oh, by the way," Sarah says, switching topics, "your mom called a million times tonight."

Jasmine's smile fades slightly, her excitement momentarily dimming. She rolls her eyes, frustration creeping into her voice.

"That old woman worries too much," she mutters, her lips forming a thin line. She loves her mom, but sometimes it feels like she's being watched from every angle, and it can be suffocating.

Sarah chuckles, a playful glint in her eye. "I was really tempted to pick up," she admits, teasingly. "But I figured it was best not to get involved."

Jasmine's face tightens, irritation flashing across her features. Her mom's constant calls, the worry she could almost feel from miles away, it all felt a little too much tonight.

"Don't you dare," she says firmly, her voice cold, but there's a flicker of worry in her eyes. "I'm on my way home now."

Sarah shakes her head, a grin spreading across her face as she gives her friend a teasing nudge. "Alright, alright, I won't be the messenger," she says, laughing. "But seriously, Jasmine, your mom's gonna freak out when she finds out what happened tonight."

Jasmine shrugs, trying to brush off the tension. She's still on cloud nine, her thoughts consumed by the evening's whirlwind, but there's a part of her that knows her mom's worry isn't going away anytime soon. Still, tonight... tonight was hers.

The two continue walking, the sounds of the party growing more distant as they make their way toward the car. For a moment, everything felt like it was in perfect balance—Sarah's laughter echoing in her ears, the world buzzing with possibilities. But beneath the surface, the familiar weight of her mom's concern lingers, threatening to pull her back to reality. But not tonight. Tonight was about something bigger, something new.

And she wasn't ready to let go of that feeling just yet.

As Sarah teasingly walks a few steps ahead, she calls back over her shoulder, "Alright, alright. Just making sure you don't get in trouble." There's a playful note in her voice, but the underlying concern is clear.

Jasmine forces a smile, though it's tinged with relief. She's glad that Sarah is giving her space, not pressing further about the details of her conversation with Trey. Jasmine knows the last thing she needs is to get caught up in another round of concerned questioning. Tonight is hers to keep, and she doesn't want anyone, not even her closest friends, to spoil it with their worries.

"I'll handle it," Jasmine assures her, the words flowing with an air of confidence that doesn't quite mask the nerves still swirling inside her. She's been managing her own problems for a while now, and she'll handle this one too. Her mom will just have to wait.

Sarah nods approvingly, giving her friend a quick, supportive hug before turning to leave. The hug is brief but warm, and for a split second, Jasmine allows herself to enjoy the simple comfort of it—something that helps anchor her amidst the chaos of the night.

As Sarah walks off, Jasmine stands still for a moment, her thoughts spinning in a hundred different directions. She watches her friend disappear into the shadows of the street, the sound of her footsteps fading into the night. A deep breath escapes her lips, and she lets the cool air fill her lungs, trying to steady herself.

The adrenaline from the party still pulses in her veins. Her mind drifts back to the conversation with Trey—the way he had looked at her, the promise of a new life, a life of possibilities that she'd never dared to imagine before. It all felt too surreal to process. One minute she was just another girl at a party, and now... now, she's on the verge of something big. Something she could never have dreamed of.

She reaches into her pocket and pulls out the sleek business card he had given her earlier. She holds it in her fingers for a moment, turning it over in her hand. The weight of it feels important, heavy with potential. The address, the time, it all echoes in her mind. She'll be at his office tomorrow, at 10 a.m., ready to take the first step toward whatever it is he's offering.

A part of her wonders if this is too much too soon. But another part—the part that had been waiting for a chance like this her whole life—can't wait to dive in headfirst. She's ready.

With one last glance at Sarah's retreating figure, Jasmine tucks the business card back into her pocket and turns toward the car. Tonight had been a whirlwind, but it was only the beginning. She was about to step into a world where everything could change.

Chapter 11

The soft light of the morning creeps through the curtains, casting a gentle glow across the room. Jasmine stirs, blinking slowly as the remnants of sleep cloud her mind. She squints at the clock on her nightstand—it's later than she intended. A groan escapes her lips as she pulls herself up into a sitting position, rubbing her eyes.

Before she can fully collect herself, the door creaks open, and her mother, Mrs. Thompson, stands there, arms crossed, her face drawn with a mixture of worry and frustration. The moment Jasmine sees her, she knows what's coming.

"Jasmine, where did you go last night?" Mrs. Thompson's voice is calm but laced with concern, her gaze never wavering from her daughter.

Jasmine feels a wave of annoyance wash over her. She's not in the mood for another lecture. The events of the night before are still fresh in her mind, but she doesn't want to get into it right now. She sits up further, scrunching her face as she shoots her mother an irritated look.

"I am no longer a child you have to look over. I was out. Period!" Her voice has an edge to it as she speaks, a mix of frustration and exhaustion creeping into her words.

Mrs. Thompson's brows furrow in a deeper expression of concern, and she steps forward, her voice softening but still filled with the same intensity. "And why didn't you pick up my calls? I've been trying to reach you all night!"

Jasmine rolls her eyes in frustration and flops back onto her pillows, burying her face in the softness of the fabric. "I want to sleep. I'm tired, Mom. Just let me be." Her tone is dismissive now, her body sinking deeper into the comfort of the bed as if hoping her mother would just drop it.

There's a long pause as Mrs. Thompson stands there, her hands still clasped tightly in front of her. She opens her mouth, as if to say something, but instead, she exhales slowly, shaking her head in resignation. She doesn't argue further, knowing that no matter what she says, Jasmine is too far into her mood to listen.

With a quiet sigh, Mrs. Thompson turns and walks out of the room, closing the door gently behind her. Jasmine hears the soft click of the latch, signaling the end of the confrontation. She remains still for a moment, letting the silence fill the room. The weight of her mother's concern still lingers, but Jasmine doesn't want to deal with it. Not today. Not after everything that happened last night.

She pulls the covers up around her, curling into a small ball as the events of the evening replay in her mind. The excitement, the rush of meeting someone like Trey, the world he had promised her—money, fame, the lifestyle. It feels like a dream, but it's one she's ready to chase. The reality of it all hasn't quite hit her yet, and for now, all she wants to do is sleep and escape the pressure of the expectations already starting to build around her.

She closes her eyes, hoping the rest of the day can wait just a little longer.

The door clicks shut behind her mother, and the lingering tension in the room begins to ease. For a brief moment, Jasmine allows herself to settle back into the bed, letting the quietness wash over her. But then, her eyes catch the time on the clock, and a sudden jolt of panic shoots through her.

"Oh no!" Her voice is filled with alarm as she sees the time: 9:30 AM. Her heart skips a beat. She's already late.

The rush of realization hits her like a tidal wave. She jumps out of bed in a hurry, her earlier irritation completely forgotten. The excitement of the night before, the conversation with Trey, and the business card he handed her all flood back into her mind.

Her heart races as she darts across the room. She doesn't have time to waste. Trey had asked her to be at his office by 10 AM, and she knows how important this could be—an opportunity she can't afford to miss. She needs to get moving. Fast.

Jasmine's movements are quick and frantic as she yanks clothes from the closet, not caring if they match or not. She's in full-on panic mode, tugging her shirt over her head with one hand while trying to shove jeans onto her legs with the other. The pressure is building with every second that ticks away, the clock ticking down like a countdown to something monumental. She can feel the weight of the moment pressing in on her.

"I've got to get to Trey's office..." she mutters to herself, her voice low but filled with determination.

Her mind races as she pulls her hair into a hasty ponytail, not bothering with any finesse. Her fingers fumble with her makeup bag, barely dabbing on some concealer and mascara, but there's no time for perfection. Her reflection in the mirror barely registers as she brushes her teeth in a hurried frenzy.

With each frantic movement, she feels both the rush of excitement and the undercurrent of anxiety building. This could be her shot, the opportunity that could change everything—fame, money, the life she's always dreamed of. But it's all happening so fast, and the clock is ticking down mercilessly.

She grabs her phone, quickly checking the time again—9:45 AM. She's going to be cutting it close.

As she darts out of the room, her mind swirls with a mix of nerves and anticipation. She doesn't have time to think about anything else, not her mom's concerns, not the consequences, just the opportunity that awaits her at Trey's office.

She runs down the stairs, her footsteps light but heavy with purpose, and before she knows it, she's out the door, already halfway to the car.

Jasmine walked through the sleek glass doors into the office, her eyes widening as she took in the luxurious surroundings. The space was modern and stylish, with high-end furnishings and artwork that exuded wealth and sophistication. The walls were lined with framed platinum records and glossy magazine covers featuring Trey.

A polished marble reception desk stood at the front, with a well-dressed receptionist seated behind it, typing on a computer.

"Good morning," the receptionist smiled, glancing up. "May I help you?"

Jasmine, feeling a mix of nerves and excitement, responded softly, "Yes, I'm Jasmine. I'm here to see Trey."

The receptionist checked her computer screen and nodded. "Of course, Miss Jasmine. He's expecting you. Please have a seat, and I'll let him know you've arrived."

Jasmine took a seat in the luxurious waiting area, her eyes roaming around the space. The plush velvet chairs, modern art sculptures, and impressive view of the city skyline through the floor-to-ceiling windows caught her attention. She couldn't help but feel both out of place and drawn to the sleek, luxurious vibe of the office. It felt like the kind of world she had only dreamed of.

Her fingers tapped nervously on her phone as her mind raced with thoughts of what this meeting could mean. Everything in this office—the polished marble, the stunning view—spoke of success and power, and for a brief moment, she wondered if she truly belonged here.

The receptionist, still typing away on the computer, didn't acknowledge Jasmine further. Jasmine tried to calm her nerves by focusing on the view outside. The city stretched endlessly below, full of possibilities, and the light filtering in through the windows gave everything a dreamlike glow. But it didn't stop her heart from beating faster, anticipation and excitement swirling within her.

After what felt like an eternity, the receptionist finally looked up, offering a warm, professional smile. "Miss Jasmine, Trey will see you now."

Jasmine's heart skipped a beat, a wave of excitement washing over her. She quickly stood, smoothing out her clothes, trying to make herself appear composed despite the racing thoughts in her mind.

A few moments later, Trey emerged from his private office, the door clicking softly behind him as he walked toward Jasmine. His presence commanded attention, and he moved with the effortless confidence of someone used to being admired. His smile was warm, yet laced with an undeniable charm, making Jasmine's heart flutter in anticipation.

"Jasmine!" he greeted, his voice smooth and welcoming. "You made it."

Jasmine stood up quickly, her pulse racing at the sight of him. She tried to keep her composure, but the excitement bubbling within her made it hard to stay cool. "Yeah, I did. Thanks for having me," she replied, her voice a little breathless but genuine.

Trey nodded approvingly and motioned for her to follow him into his office. His long stride was purposeful, and Jasmine couldn't help but feel a sense of awe as she trailed behind him. The office doors were grand, opening into a space that spoke of success and sophistication. Jasmine's gaze immediately swept over the room, her eyes widening as she took in the opulence.

The office was designed to impress. Rich mahogany furniture gave the room a sense of power, while sleek, modern accents added a touch of luxury. Behind a large, polished desk sat an executive chair that looked more like a throne, the kind you only saw in high-end magazines. Floor-to-ceiling bookshelves lined the walls, stacked with leather-bound books, framed awards, and a dazzling array of gold and platinum records. Each one gleamed under the soft lighting, telling the story of Trey's accomplishments. The room had an elegant, almost intimidating atmosphere, as if every detail had been carefully curated to project a sense of dominance and wealth.

Trey gestured toward a plush leather sofa across from the desk, his smile widening. "Please, have a seat. We'll go over everything."

Jasmine glanced at the sofa before lowering herself onto it. The leather was cool against her skin, and the plush cushions enveloped her, almost too comfortable for the serious conversation ahead. Her heart pounded in her chest as she tried to steady her breath, aware of how big this moment was. This was the opportunity she had been dreaming of, and now that she was here, her mind raced with what came next.

Trey moved to sit behind his desk, his presence still commanding the space. The chair creaked slightly as he settled into it, his posture impeccable. He wasted no time pulling out a sleek tablet, swiping through the screen with practiced ease, and laid down a few documents in front of him. His eyes briefly flicked up to meet hers, that confident, magnetic smile still in place.

"So, Jasmine," he began, his tone steady and assured. "Let's talk about how we're going to make you a star." He leaned forward slightly, the excitement in his eyes matching hers. "I've got some exciting plans for you."

Jasmine felt a rush of energy surge through her. This was it— the chance she had been waiting for. She was no longer just a hopeful girl dreaming from the sidelines. She was here, in this beautiful office, being told she had what it took to become a star. Her heart swelled with a mixture of disbelief and excitement, and she found herself smiling without even thinking about it.

"Tell me more," she said, her voice tinged with eagerness.

Trey's grin deepened as he began to explain his vision, and Jasmine leaned in, hanging on to every word.

As Trey leans back in his chair, his smile is almost predatory, but there's a softness in his eyes that makes his words feel more personal. His gaze lingers on Jasmine a little too long, and she can't help but feel the weight of his attention.

Trey flips through a few more documents, but his focus has clearly shifted from business to something else. He looks up at her with that same calculating yet admiring smile.

"You know, Jasmine," he says, his voice smooth and measured, "while we're discussing your career, I have to say... I couldn't help but notice how stunning you are. The moment I saw you, it was like seeing a dream come to life."

Jasmine, caught off guard by the unexpected compliment, suppresses a reaction. She raises an eyebrow, keeping her voice casual as she responds, trying to keep the situation under control.

"Oh, really? Thanks," she says, offering him a polite smile, but inside she's already trying to mentally distance herself from his words. This is a professional meeting, and she refuses to let it veer off course.

Trey's smile deepens, his gaze growing more intense. He leans forward, a calculated move, his tone dropping to something more intimate, more personal.

"I mean it," he continues, his voice thick with sincerity. "You're more than just a pretty face. I've dreamt about someone like you. I'd love for you to be more than just a part of my music."

Jasmine's eyes widen slightly at the unexpected shift in tone. She feels a jolt of discomfort, but she hides it well. Her mind races, but she keeps her expression neutral, not wanting to show any weakness. Trey was a powerful figure in the industry, and she needed to stay focused on what brought her here: her career.

That moment of hesitation is all he needs, and he leans in closer, his intentions growing clearer. His proximity is too much. Jasmine's heart skips a beat, but she quickly raises her hand, gently but firmly stopping him from getting any closer.

"Let's keep this professional," Jasmine says softly, but with enough authority in her voice to make her point clear. Her fingers curl slightly as if bracing herself, though she's trying to remain calm.

Trey hesitates for just a moment, a flicker of surprise crossing his face. His smile falters but doesn't disappear entirely. He leans back slightly in his chair, still watching her, but now more guarded.

"Of course," he says, the charm in his voice slipping back into place. "I respect that. We'll keep things professional, Jasmine. Just know that I think you've got incredible potential—both as an artist and, well... in other ways, too."

Jasmine nods firmly, relieved that he seems to have backed off for now, but the unsettling feeling lingers. She forces a smile, though it's more out of politeness than genuine enjoyment.

"Let's stick to the career plans, then," she says, a slight edge in her voice as she steers the conversation back on track.

Trey nods, clearly sensing that any further personal talk would not be welcomed. He picks up the documents again, his focus returning to business.

"Right," he says smoothly. "Let's talk about your future in this industry, Jasmine."

Trey pulls back, his smile faltering for just a moment, before he regains his composure. He stares at her for a brief second, his expression shifting into one of understanding, though there's a hint of disappointment that lingers in his eyes. Without saying much more, he reaches into his desk drawer and pulls out a check, the thick paper making a slight rustling sound as he smooths it across the desk.

With a swift motion, he writes something on the check with a flourish, his pen moving with ease. He looks up at Jasmine with a sincere gaze, his voice calm but still carrying that underlying charm.

"I respect that," he says, his tone genuine. "Here, take this. Consider it an advance on your future with us."

He slides the check toward her, and Jasmine's eyes widen in disbelief. She slowly reaches for it, her fingers trembling slightly as she picks it up. The large sum written on the check takes her breath away, her heart racing with excitement.

Her eyes flicker between the check and Trey, and she can't help herself—she screams with excitement, her voice filled with sheer joy.

"Oh my God! This is amazing!" she exclaims, her voice high-pitched with enthusiasm.

Trey's smile widens, pleased with her reaction, his eyes gleaming as he watches her. "I'm glad you're happy," he says, his tone warm. "How about we celebrate this opportunity with a date tonight? Just the two of us."

Jasmine's heart skips a beat, her mind racing with the possibilities that now lie before her. She grins widely, unable to suppress the excitement bubbling up inside her.

"I'd love that!" she replies, her voice practically dripping with enthusiasm.

Trey nods approvingly, clearly pleased with her response. Jasmine stands up from the sofa, still clutching the check tightly in her hand. The weight of the moment is overwhelming, but her grin never fades as she meets Trey's gaze.

"I'll pick you up at seven," Trey says, his voice smooth as always. "See you then, Jasmine."

Jasmine nods eagerly, her eyes sparkling with the kind of excitement that only a life-changing moment could bring. "Definitely. See you tonight!"

With that, she exits the office, the door clicking softly behind her. As she walks down the sleek hallway, the check still clutched tightly in her hand, her mind is buzzing with the thrill of the night ahead. The promise of both wealth and the allure of a romantic evening fills her thoughts, and she can hardly contain her excitement as she imagines what the future may hold.

Chapter 12

As the days passed, their meetings became more frequent, more spontaneous, and increasingly unprofessional. What had started as business encounters, brief discussions, and professional exchanges, gradually morphed into something more personal and intimate. Trey, once all business, now made it a point to carve out time for Jasmine outside of the office, suggesting casual meetups, dinner dates, and walks in the park. Each encounter seemed to blur the lines between their professional relationship and a more personal connection, neither of them quite willing to acknowledge it yet, but both feeling it more with every passing day.

One evening, they found themselves seated at an upscale restaurant, the soft glow of candlelight dancing in their eyes as the sound of jazz floated in the background. Trey, dressed sharply in a tailored suit, leaned in closer than necessary, his gaze locking onto Jasmine's with an intensity that left her heart racing. They shared a delicious meal, their laughter ringing through the air, but there was more than just the meal; there was a magnetic pull between them that neither could ignore.

Trey's compliments were more than just polite praise. "You're not just beautiful, Jasmine. You're captivating. Every time I'm around you, I can't look away," he said, his words both flattering and loaded with something deeper. Jasmine, usually quick-witted, found herself speechless, the words settling between them like a heavy perfume.

Despite the lingering tension, Jasmine smiled, hiding her growing unease behind her drink, but the warmth creeping into her cheeks betrayed her. She tried to dismiss the compliments, keeping her responses light and casual, but there was no denying the chemistry between them. Each word, each glance, each touch seemed to pull them closer, threading their worlds together in a way that was anything but professional.

The next day, they met again, this time in the city's park. The atmosphere was lighter, more relaxed, but there was still an undercurrent of something more. As they strolled hand in hand through the sun-dappled paths, past families with children and dogs playing in the distance, their conversation drifted from business to personal. Trey asked about Jasmine's childhood, about her dreams, and the carefree days of youth she sometimes longed for. Jasmine, caught off guard by the question, found herself answering in ways she hadn't expected. They shared a quiet moment, her head resting gently on his shoulder as they walked, the world around them fading into the background.

Trey pulled out his phone, snapping pictures of Jasmine with a tenderness that felt out of place in their business relationship. The photos weren't just about capturing moments; they were about capturing her—her laughter, her smile, the way the light played in her hair. As they paused for a moment, Trey kissed her forehead lightly, a gesture that, while innocent, spoke volumes about the growing intimacy between them.

Their interactions had shifted, moving from professional discussions to personal exchanges, and neither of them was particularly concerned about it. The line that once separated business from pleasure had all but disappeared, replaced by something else—something neither could fully define but both were beginning to feel with increasing clarity. Despite Jasmine's initial hesitation and attempts to keep things professional, the connection between them was undeniable, and every meeting only deepened the bond that was forming between them.

As the days turned into weeks, their meetings took on a life of their own, becoming increasingly intimate and blurred between professional and personal. It wasn't just about contracts or career moves anymore. Jasmine found herself drawn deeper into Trey's world, a world of luxury and allure that had once felt like something out of a dream.

One afternoon, Trey invited her to his luxurious home, and Jasmine couldn't hide her awe as they walked through his grand living room. The space was open and expansive, bathed in natural light, with elegant furniture and tasteful decor. The floor-to-ceiling windows offered a breathtaking view of the city skyline. Jasmine's eyes widened as she took in the view, a mixture of admiration and disbelief on her face.

Trey, noticing her amazement, couldn't help but smile. He casually gestured to the art pieces hanging on the walls, each one more striking than the last. "These are some of my favorites," Trey said, his voice soft, but with an edge of pride. "Art's always been a way for me to express myself, even when words fail." Jasmine leaned in, admiring the bold strokes of color and the abstract shapes, and they began discussing their favorites. Their conversation was light-hearted, filled with playful banter and laughter, but there was an undeniable spark in the air between them.

As the tour continued, Jasmine felt an increasing warmth and connection with Trey, one that she couldn't easily explain. The casual nature of their exchanges began to fade into something more tender, more personal.

Later that night, the setting shifted once again. Trey's bedroom, bathed in soft, golden light, felt like an intimate cocoon, away from the busy world outside. The city lights filtered through the curtains, casting gentle shadows on the walls. Trey and Jasmine stood close, their bodies inching toward each other as their breaths mingled in the cool night air.

There, under the muted glow of the room, they shared a quiet, tender kiss. It was soft and slow, a kiss that lingered with unspoken emotions. Their silhouettes were the only things visible, framed against the backdrop of the vast city below. For a moment, it felt as if nothing else mattered—no contracts, no career ambitions, just the feeling of being in each other's arms.

The kiss deepened slightly, but there was an awareness between them, a shift from their earlier playful moments. Jasmine felt a rush of warmth and desire that she couldn't ignore, but there was still a hesitation, a lingering thought at the back of her mind reminding her of the fine line they were walking. Despite that, the kiss, the intimacy, felt undeniable.

As their connection deepened, their time together became increasingly relaxed, yet undeniably intimate. The professional boundaries that once defined their meetings seemed to fade, replaced by moments that felt more like the easy comfort of a couple rather than two people simply working together.

One evening, they curled up on the couch in Trey's living room, wrapped in a soft, cozy blanket. The atmosphere was relaxed, with the glow of the TV screen casting a gentle light across the room. They shared a bowl of popcorn, occasionally feeding each other, their laughter filling the air in between moments of quiet enjoyment. Jasmine's head rested on Trey's shoulder, the warmth of his body pressing against hers, as they both lost themselves in the movie. Every so often, their eyes would meet, and without a word, a gentle kiss would follow. It felt effortless, a simple pleasure that made their bond feel all the more real.

A few days later, they found themselves on the rooftop of a chic bar, the city's twinkling lights stretching out beneath them like a sea of stars. Trey and Jasmine stood close together, leaning against the railing, sipping on cocktails as the cool breeze ruffled their hair. They spoke animatedly, their conversation a mixture of laughter and shared thoughts, with Trey occasionally glancing down at Jasmine, his arm wrapping around her waist. The warmth of his embrace seemed to hold her in place, her head resting against his chest as they took in the view.

Later that week, they visited an art gallery together, a space filled with vibrant displays of creativity. Jasmine's eyes lit up as they moved from one exhibit to the next, discussing the meaning behind certain pieces and the emotions they evoked. Trey stood close by, listening intently, offering his own thoughts and drawing her into deeper conversation. They paused in front of a particularly moving painting, and Jasmine shared her interpretation of it with such passion that Trey couldn't help but be captivated by both her insight and the energy she exuded. They exchanged glances that were filled with more than just appreciation for art; there was an unspoken understanding between them that felt more intimate than any words could express. As Jasmine's hand brushed against his, Trey's fingers lingered for a moment before they intertwined, an easy, natural gesture of connection.

Their growing bond continued to unfold in the most beautiful and spontaneous ways, each moment feeling like a chapter in a love story that neither of them expected but both cherished deeply.

One evening, they found themselves on a secluded beach, walking barefoot along the soft sand as the sun began its descent. The sky exploded in shades of gold, pink, and purple, reflecting off the water like a painted canvas. The rhythmic sound of the waves crashing gently against the shore added a tranquil soundtrack to the moment. As they walked hand in hand, Trey pulled Jasmine closer, his gaze softening as he looked into her eyes. Without a word, he leaned in and pressed his lips against hers in a gentle, lingering kiss. The warmth of the sunset and the tenderness of the kiss made everything feel timeless, as if the world had slowed down just for them.

The following morning, the sun streamed through the windows of Trey's kitchen, casting a golden glow over everything. The kitchen was bright and cheerful, filled with the scent of sizzling ingredients. Trey and Jasmine worked side by side, preparing breakfast together, their movements synchronized in a playful harmony. Jasmine stirred the pan with a grin, while Trey set the table, his eyes constantly flicking over to her with a mixture of amusement and affection. Their banter was lighthearted, filled with laughter as they playfully tossed ingredients at each other, causing more than one small mess. The air was thick with warmth and joy. Before sitting down to eat, they exchanged a quick kiss, a moment of shared happiness that felt like the perfect way to start the day.

Their connection deepened with each passing moment, and the more time they spent together, the more their bond flourished in the simplest of moments, far away from the world's expectations.

On a bright, serene afternoon, they decided to spend the day in a peaceful park. The grass was soft beneath them, and the air carried the faint scent of blooming flowers. They lay side by side on a picnic blanket, the warmth of the sun gently enveloping them as they both relaxed in each other's presence. Trey, ever the romantic, pulled out his guitar and began to play a soft, melodic tune. His fingers moved with practiced ease over the strings, creating a sound that seemed to flow in harmony with the tranquil surroundings. Jasmine closed her eyes, the peaceful music washing over her. She rested her head in his lap, her hair fanning out on the soft fabric of the blanket. The world around them felt distant, as if time itself had paused just for them. Every now and then, Trey would stop playing to lean down and kiss Jasmine softly on the forehead or cheek, a tender gesture that spoke volumes more than words could. They exchanged quiet, intimate kisses, each one lingering longer than the last, while the afternoon unfolded peacefully around them. There was an unspoken comfort in the silence they shared, a mutual understanding that needed no explanation. The gentle breeze rustled the leaves of nearby trees, but all they could focus on was each other, lost in the moment and the beauty of the world they had created together.

Later that night, after a long and fulfilling day, Trey and Jasmine found themselves on the couch in the warmth of Trey's living room. The space was dimly lit by the flickering light of the television, which cast gentle shadows on their faces. The soft hum of the TV blended with the quiet rustle of the blanket they were wrapped in. Jasmine's head was nestled comfortably against Trey's chest, her hair resting on the fabric of his shirt as she listened to the steady rhythm of his heartbeat. Her eyes were closed in contentment, her body relaxing further into his embrace with each passing second. The movie played on, but neither of them paid much attention to the plot, their focus entirely on the moment. The world outside seemed irrelevant; it was just the two of them, their closeness, the warmth of the blanket, and the intimacy of the moment that made everything else fade away. Trey absentmindedly brushed a lock of hair away from her face, his fingers tracing the curve of her jaw as she sighed softly. The quiet intimacy of the scene was comforting, their hearts beating in sync, as if time had stopped in the presence of this shared connection.

Occasionally, Trey would shift his position slightly, pulling the blanket tighter around them, his arm securely wrapped around her shoulders as if to protect and cherish her in that quiet, peaceful space. There was something deeply satisfying about this simplicity, this moment of calm, where nothing else mattered except the closeness they shared, the love that filled the room without a single word spoken.

Jasmine stepped through the front door, her heels clicking against the polished hardwood floor, and the large designer bag hanging from her shoulder swayed with every stride. She was dressed in a way that would turn heads—her clothes were sleek, trendy, and flawlessly coordinated. Her hair cascaded down in perfectly styled waves, and she exuded an effortless aura of confidence and beauty. She took a deep breath as she stepped into the familiar, quiet space of her house. It was a house that, despite the opulence, always seemed to lack warmth. Her footsteps echoed in the empty hallway, and she was about to head upstairs when she noticed her mother standing in the living room, holding a small, elegantly wrapped gift box in her hands.

Mrs. Thompson, dressed in a modest but elegant outfit, was staring at her daughter with an expression that could only be described as both concerned and expectant. She had always been the type of mother who cared deeply for Jasmine, yet there was a persistent disconnect between them—one that had only grown more noticeable as Jasmine's life became more centered around the fast-paced world she now inhabited.

As soon as Jasmine entered the living room, Mrs. Thompson looked up from the small box she had been examining, her gaze filled with a mix of curiosity and something else, something that seemed to be a longing for a connection that Jasmine rarely offered.

"Jasmine, where have you been?" Mrs. Thompson's voice was soft, but there was an underlying edge of worry, as if she had been waiting for her daughter to come home.

Jasmine paused just inside the living room, the cool indifference in her posture as evident as ever. Her eyes briefly flicked to her mother, and then she shrugged nonchalantly, dropping her designer bag onto the nearby couch without much care. "Please, I'm not ready for this," she said, her voice sharp and laced with irritation.

Mrs. Thompson furrowed her brow, noticing her daughter's tone, but she pushed forward, unwilling to let the moment slip away without addressing something that had been bothering her. "Your friend came by earlier," she began, her words measured. "He mentioned he knows you from way back… preschool or so. Why didn't you tell me about this?"

Jasmine rolled her eyes, clearly uninterested in continuing the conversation. She sighed dramatically, tossing her hair back with a quick motion and looking at her mother like she was burdened by the mere question. "How many times do I have to tell you that Marcus is not my friend?" she snapped, a trace of annoyance thickening her words. "And I don't think that information about knowing me from way back matters."

Mrs. Thompson blinked, taken aback by the sharpness of Jasmine's reply. She was starting to recognize the walls her daughter had built around herself—walls that had only gotten higher with time. But Mrs. Thompson, ever the hopeful mother, wasn't ready to give up. "I just thought—" she started, but before she could finish, Jasmine's attention shifted.

Jasmine's gaze drifted to the small gift box her mother was still holding. She had barely even acknowledged it until now, but the sight of it caused a sudden unease to settle in her stomach. It was a beautifully wrapped package, and her mother's expression suggested she was expecting a different kind of reaction.

Mrs. Thompson gently opened the box and pulled out a delicate bracelet, its shining silver band adorned with small, shimmering stones. "He brought this for you," Mrs. Thompson said softly, her voice tinged with a hope that Jasmine might, for once, respond with some measure of appreciation. "I thought you might like it."

Jasmine's eyes flickered with something like disdain, and without even glancing properly at the bracelet, she flicked her wrist dismissively, causing the bracelet to fall from her mother's hands. It landed with a soft clatter on the floor, the metallic sound echoing in the otherwise quiet room.

"I don't need this crap," Jasmine muttered under her breath, her voice barely above a whisper but filled with venom. She didn't even look at her mother as she spoke, her body already moving toward the stairs.

Mrs. Thompson's face crumpled, a mixture of hurt and disbelief washing over her features. She looked at the bracelet on the floor, then back at her daughter, her voice trembling as she spoke. "Jasmine, that's not how you treat people," she said, her tone soft but laced with disappointment.

But Jasmine, unbothered, didn't even pause. She didn't feel the need to defend herself or explain her actions. Her mother's words barely seemed to reach her. "Whatever," she muttered, her voice cold and sharp as she turned away. "I'm going out."

She didn't wait for her mother's response as she stormed up the stairs, her footsteps loud and deliberate, as if marking a boundary she never intended to cross. Mrs. Thompson stood there, holding the small gift box in her hands, the bracelet now forgotten on the floor. She sighed softly, her heart sinking at the growing distance between her and her daughter. The silence in the house grew heavier, and the once-welcoming atmosphere now felt distant and cold.

Jasmine didn't look back.

Chapter 13

Jasmine emerged from her room, and the transformation was undeniable. Gone was the casual, laid-back outfit she had worn earlier. In its place was a bold, eye-catching ensemble that could have been plucked straight from a music video shoot. Her tight-fitting leather jacket glinted under the hallway lights, paired with sleek black boots that gave her an undeniable edge. The short skirt she wore highlighted her long legs, and her makeup was fierce, with dark eyeliner accentuating her sharp features. Her hair, once flowing in waves, was now styled to perfection, each strand meticulously placed. The contrast was jarring—this was not the same girl who had stormed up the stairs earlier in frustration. This was a new version of Jasmine, one that exuded confidence, power, and a touch of rebellion.

She moved with purpose, her heels clicking decisively on the wooden floor as she headed towards the front door. Mrs. Thompson stood at the doorframe, her expression filled with a mixture of concern and confusion, watching as her daughter approached. Jasmine paused for a brief moment, her eyes meeting her mother's with an unmistakable smirk—a gesture that seemed to hold both defiance and something else, something almost like excitement.

"Where are you going?" Mrs. Thompson's voice trembled slightly, her concern evident as she tried to read the situation.

Jasmine's eyes sparkled with an energy that almost felt too intense, as though she were living in her own world where nothing else mattered. She shrugged, her smirk turning into a confident grin. "I've got something important to take care of. Big plans tonight," she said with a nonchalant air, her tone filled with a sense of mystery and something like exhilaration.

Before Mrs. Thompson could ask more questions or voice her concerns, Jasmine was already turning, reaching for the door handle. The sound of the door clicking open seemed to echo in the otherwise quiet house, and without another word, Jasmine stepped out.

Mrs. Thompson stood there for a moment, her heart sinking. She watched as Jasmine made her way toward the front yard, her heels tapping rhythmically against the pavement. Her daughter's bold stride was filled with purpose, and despite the overwhelming worry clouding her mind, Mrs. Thompson couldn't help but feel a pang of fear for what her daughter's plans might entail.

Jasmine's luxurious car was waiting at the curb—a sleek, black sedan that stood out against the suburban backdrop. The driver, a man she had never seen before, opened the door for her, his face polite but distant. Jasmine slid into the car with the grace of someone who had done this a thousand times. The door clicked shut behind her, and the car smoothly pulled away, leaving Mrs. Thompson standing there in the doorway, a mixture of concern, confusion, and a nagging feeling of helplessness washing over her.

She watched as the car disappeared down the street, her mind racing with thoughts she couldn't quite put together. Was Jasmine truly ready for whatever she was headed toward? And if not, what would happen when she realized that the choices she was making could lead her down a dangerous path?

Mrs. Thompson stood frozen, her heart heavy with the weight of uncertainty. The quiet house seemed to close in around her, amplifying her feelings of isolation and worry. She had hoped for more time to guide Jasmine, to help her see the consequences of her actions, but now, it felt as though her daughter was slipping further and further away from her grasp.

The luxury mansion stood tall, bathed in the golden sunlight, its pristine walls and expansive grounds offering a picturesque backdrop to the bustling music video set. Crew members darted around, adjusting lights, positioning cameras, and testing sound equipment, all under the pressure of the fast-approaching start time. The air was thick with a sense of urgency, but it didn't seem to faze Jasmine. She strode onto the set with an air of entitlement, her every step deliberate and full of purpose.

Her outfit caught the light in all the right ways—a shimmering ensemble that sparkled with each movement, emphasizing her figure and drawing eyes. The designer clothes she wore screamed opulence, a reflection of the persona she had carefully crafted. Her heels clicked against the marble floor as she moved, and the set seemed to momentarily pause around her, as though everyone instinctively knew to step aside for the star of the show.

Jasmine's chin was held high, her posture exuding confidence, perhaps even arrogance, as she walked past the crew members scrambling to get things in order. She didn't acknowledge them, barely even sparing a glance, her eyes focused on herself and the image she wanted to project.

An assistant, looking a little flustered, approached cautiously, trying to catch her attention as she made her way toward the center of the set. "Jasmine," the assistant said politely, her voice edged with professionalism but also the hint of nervousness. "Can I get you anything before we start?"

Jasmine didn't even look at her, her gaze straight ahead as she adjusted the collar of her jacket. She waved the assistant off with a flick of her hand, her voice dripping with disdain. "I'm good. Just make sure the lighting's perfect, alright?" she said, her words sharp and dismissive. "I'm not about to look average on camera."

The assistant nodded quickly, retreating to her station, but Jasmine's words lingered in the air. Her tone had been so cold, so assured, that it left no room for further discussion. The crew, no strangers to celebrity attitudes, continued their work, but there was a subtle shift in the atmosphere. Jasmine wasn't just a star here—she was the queen, and everyone else was just a part of the machine that kept her in the spotlight.

With a satisfied glance around the set, Jasmine adjusted her outfit again, smoothing out the fabric as if she were preparing for battle. Every angle, every detail had to be perfect. This wasn't just a music video; this was her moment, and she was determined to make sure it would be remembered. The vanity mirrors around the room reflected her flawless image, and she couldn't help but smile, a self-satisfied smirk playing on her lips. She was in her element now, the center of attention, and she was ready to show the world just how much power she held.

The pool area was transformed into a glitzy, glamorous setting for the music video shoot. The sun shone brightly, casting a golden glow over the turquoise water and sparkling tiles around the pool. Luxurious loungers were scattered across the deck, and sparkling champagne flutes rested on small tables, giving the scene an indulgent atmosphere. A soft breeze rustled through the palm trees surrounding the area, but the energy on set was anything but relaxed. The crew hustled around, setting up cameras, adjusting lighting, and coordinating last-minute tweaks.

Jasmine stood at the center of the pool area, the focal point of the entire shoot. Her sparkling, skin-tight outfit clung to her body, catching the light with every move she made. Around her, a group of other dancers and models flanked her, all in matching outfits, their faces painted with confidence and seduction. But even amidst this sea of beauty, Jasmine was the undeniable star. Her poise, her presence—everything about her demanded attention.

The director, positioned behind the camera, signaled for the music to start. The upbeat, thumping rhythm filled the air, and the mood instantly shifted. The cameras rolled, and the dancers sprang into action, moving in sync with the beat. Jasmine, however, was playing a different game altogether. As the music thumped louder, her hips swayed, and she began twerking with exaggerated flair. Each movement was calculated—sharp, precise, and designed to keep every camera lens glued to her. Her eyes flickered to the monitors briefly, noticing how the cameras were zooming in on her, focusing on her every step.

The other dancers tried to keep up, but it was obvious that they were merely background noise compared to Jasmine's electrifying energy. As they attempted to mirror the choreography, Jasmine threw in extra moves—twisting her body with extra sass, arching her back with intentional exaggeration, and throwing in spins that had the crowd's eyes locked solely on her.

She knew exactly what she was doing. Every twerk, every swing of her hips, every flick of her fingers was a message: I am the star. Jasmine knew how to dominate the camera. It wasn't enough to dance well; she had to ensure that nothing and no one could outshine her. And so, she became a whirlwind of energy and attitude, making the other girls seem almost invisible.

One of the dancers, slightly offbeat and trying desperately to stay in the frame, accidentally bumped into Jasmine. The moment stopped. The rhythm was lost. Jasmine froze, mid-twerk, the smile she'd been wearing fading into a cool, calculating expression. Slowly, she turned her head, her eyes narrowing in irritation as she locked eyes with the girl who had dared to disrupt her perfect performance.

The dancer looked down, immediately embarrassed, her face flushing red as she apologized, muttering something about keeping her distance. But Jasmine wasn't in the mood for an apology. She wanted to remind everyone who was in charge here.

With a tilt of her head and a raised eyebrow, Jasmine spoke in a tone dripping with mockery, her voice laced with sharp sarcasm. "Seriously?" she began, her words slow and deliberate. "You can't even stay in your lane?" She shook her head dramatically, adding a sarcastic little giggle as she continued, "Maybe dancing isn't your thing, sweetie." Her words hit like a punch, and the dancer shrank back even further, not daring to make eye contact again.

Jasmine rolled her eyes, the epitome of exasperation. "I mean, c'mon," she muttered under her breath, "how hard is it to keep up?" Her voice was just loud enough for the crew to hear, making it clear to everyone in the area that she wasn't in the mood for mistakes. Her icy glare lingered for a moment longer before she snapped her focus back to the camera.

Her stance immediately softened as she flipped her hair with an exaggerated toss, the strands swirling around her face in slow motion, making sure every eye was on her. She tilted her head up, shoulders back, chest out, and struck a pose—her signature, attention-grabbing move. With one fluid motion, she returned to the choreography, her confidence renewed and her presence unwavering.

The camera crew adjusted to catch every angle, and Jasmine gave them exactly what they wanted—more glamour, more attitude, and more star power. The other dancers quickly tried to recover, but it was clear the spotlight wasn't theirs to share.

Jasmine knew the game she was playing. The whole set was hers to command, and she wasn't about to let anyone or anything threaten that. With each beat, each flick of her hips, and each turn of her head, she reminded everyone on that set just who was in control of this show.

The director's voice echoed through the set, barely audible over the music blaring through the speakers. "Uh, Jasmine, could you move a bit to the left for this shot?" The request was polite, almost tentative, as the director tried to maintain some semblance of control over the chaotic, fast-paced atmosphere.

Jasmine, mid-motion, froze in her tracks. Her body remained perfectly still as she shot the director an incredulous look, clearly unamused by the interruption. Her lips curled into a tight, almost mocking smile, and she lifted an eyebrow as if questioning the very nerve of the request.

"Move to the left?" she repeated, her voice dripping with sarcasm. "No, I think I'm good right here," she added, with an exaggerated gesture as if to emphasize that she was more than capable of making this shot work from her position. She took a step closer to the camera as she continued, making sure to speak loudly enough for everyone to hear. "If you want the shot to be good, you'll figure it out. I'm not here to be a background extra." The words hung in the air, each syllable laced with an arrogance that made it clear Jasmine was fully aware of her importance in the scene.

The director, caught off guard, hesitated. He quickly exchanged a glance with a couple of the crew members, a silent conversation passing between them as they weighed how to handle the diva like behavior. The tension was palpable, but they were all too familiar with Jasmine's reputation. Her attitude was part of the package, and despite the discomfort it caused, they had to work with it.

Trying to maintain some semblance of professionalism, the director let out a small, defeated sigh and nodded to the camera operator. "Alright, just… adjust the angle," he muttered, waving his hand in a half-hearted gesture toward the crew. The camera operator, looking slightly hesitant but obedient, repositioned the camera to capture the shot from a different angle that still included Jasmine in the frame.

Jasmine, satisfied with her display of dominance, smirked and returned to her position, now intentionally exaggerating her movements to make sure all eyes remained on her. She could sense the tension in the air and reveled in it. She was in control—of the set, of the shot, and of how everything played out around her. She had no intention of being anyone's secondary subject. If the director wanted her to shift, it was going to have to be on her terms.

As the music resumed and the shoot continued, Jasmine's confidence never wavered. With every step, every dance move, and every look toward the camera, she reinforced her place as the star of this production, not just in the literal sense, but in the way everyone—crew, dancers, and even the director—had to dance around her needs, no matter how demanding or unreasonable they might be.

The crew bustled around the expansive living room, quickly shifting lights, adjusting cameras, and preparing for the next scene. The room was a study in luxury—high ceilings, plush velvet sofas, and walls adorned with massive, framed art pieces that gave the space a sense of sophistication. The grand chandelier hanging from the center of the ceiling sparkled in the ambient light, casting delicate shadows across the polished marble floors. The air was thick with the scent of fresh flowers, adding to the atmosphere of opulence that surrounded them.

Jasmine walked in, her steps purposeful, as if she were the queen of the mansion itself. She barely acknowledged the crew as she entered, eyes sweeping over the luxurious room with a hint of disdain, her gaze as if to say that this wasn't even impressive enough to meet her high standards. Her presence commanded attention, her confidence making her seem like she belonged in this world effortlessly.

A makeup artist, hustling to keep pace with the shoot's relentless demands, approached her cautiously with a powder puff in hand. "Just a quick powder, Jasmine. You're looking great," she said, trying to remain professional but clearly nervous under Jasmine's imposing demeanor.

Jasmine barely spared a glance at the makeup artist, her gaze flitting past her as though she were an insignificant part of the background. Her lips curled into a small, self-assured smile, and she glanced at her reflection in the mirror only momentarily before speaking. "Of course I'm looking great," she said, her voice dripping with an air of superiority. "I always do."

The makeup artist smiled awkwardly, her movements becoming quicker as she finished the touch-up, eager to avoid drawing too much attention. Jasmine was already moving on, her gaze no longer lingering on her reflection, as though the concept of perfection was a natural state for her—one that didn't require the validation of anyone else. She was confident, perhaps too confident, but that was the image she was selling, and it suited her just fine.

As the makeup artist finished, Jasmine turned, her body language emanating a quiet authority. She straightened her outfit, running a hand through her hair to ensure every strand was perfectly in place. She wasn't just the star of the shoot—she was the star of the entire production. Everyone here was just playing a supporting role to her main act.

The makeup artist backed away, her task complete, but Jasmine remained unbothered by the brief interaction. She strode toward the center of the room, her heels clicking loudly against the marble floor, each step in time with her thoughts that only focused on how she would dominate the next shot. The crew worked in the background, moving quickly to set up, aware that Jasmine's demands could be as high-maintenance as her demeanor. But no one dared challenge her—not when the cameras were rolling, and she was the one people tuned in to watch.

Jasmine's eyes narrow as she spots GIRL #2, a newer model who had yet to fully grasp her place in the hierarchy of the shoot. The girl, trying to find her spot in the scene, hesitated as she stepped forward, clearly unsure of where to position herself. Jasmine observed her with a calculating gaze, her eyes narrowing as the girl made the mistake of stepping too close to what Jasmine considered her territory.

The girl looked at her, a nervous smile forming on her lips. "I think this is where I'm supposed to stand?" she asked, her voice laced with uncertainty, unaware that she was entering dangerous territory.

Jasmine's posture stiffened, her expression shifting into one of cold, unspoken authority. She took a step forward, closing the distance between them in a move so deliberate it could not be mistaken for anything other than a power play. The air seemed to freeze as Jasmine moved into the girl's personal space, her gaze locked on her with the intensity of a predator eyeing its prey.

"No," Jasmine replied, her voice frosty, her tone sharp enough to slice through the tension in the air. "That's where I'm supposed to stand. And trust me, you don't want to compete with me for camera time." She paused, letting her words hang in the air, her eyes never leaving the girl's face. "You'd lose," she added with a mocking smirk, her confidence practically oozing from every word.

The girl blinked, her face flushing with embarrassment as she realized she had overstepped. She took a hesitant step back, clearly intimidated by Jasmine's icy demeanor and the weight of her words. Her shoulders slumped slightly, and she lowered her gaze, as if trying to make herself as small as possible in the face of Jasmine's dominance.

Jasmine, completely unphased by the girl's reaction, straightened her posture and moved confidently into the spot she had claimed as her own. She held herself like she owned the entire scene, exuding an aura of superiority that made it impossible for anyone to challenge her. She surveyed the crew briefly, then snapped her fingers, the sharp sound breaking through the tense atmosphere and drawing the attention of the production team.

"Is everything ready yet?" she asked, her voice laced with impatience. The crew immediately scrambled to adjust their equipment, the slight tremor in their hands betraying their awareness of the power Jasmine wielded on set. Everyone was focused on getting the shot perfect for her, just as she liked it. No one dared to take their eyes off her for too long, knowing that she demanded nothing less than perfection—and they would deliver, or risk falling out of her favor.

As the crew hustled to make sure everything was set up exactly to her liking, Jasmine couldn't help but smirk inwardly. This was her world, and everyone else was just living in it.

Jasmine stood in the center of the room, her posture perfect, her eyes scanning the set with an air of superiority. The crew bustled around her, making last-minute adjustments, but none of them could avoid the weight of her presence. She had already made it clear—she was the star, and everything here revolved around her. Her gaze settled on the director, who was trying to regain control of the situation after her earlier remark.

With a smile that didn't quite reach her eyes, Jasmine tilted her head slightly, the corners of her lips curving up in an expression of calculated sweetness.

"Let's make this quick," she said, her voice sweet but cutting. "I've got places to be, and I'm not wasting my time for amateurs."

Her words rang through the room, cutting off any potential objections. The crew exchanged looks, already aware of her impatience, but no one dared to challenge her. The director shifted uncomfortably, trying to gather himself, before he cleared his throat and spoke.

"Uh, we're almost set up, just give us a minute…"

Jasmine didn't respond immediately, letting the silence hang in the air. Her eyes remained fixed on the director for a beat longer than necessary, studying him as if he were an inconvenience. Then, with a slow, deliberate smile that was both condescending and gracious, she waved her hand dismissively.

"I said, let's make it quick," she repeated, the sweetness in her voice now laced with an edge of impatience. "I don't have all day."

The director swallowed hard, quickly signaling to the crew to speed things up. Lights were adjusted, cameras repositioned, and the hustle around her continued, but it was clear that Jasmine was no longer waiting for anyone.

With a confident stride, she moved to her designated spot, positioning herself perfectly for the shot. Her eyes scanned the room one last time, ensuring that everything was just as she wanted it. It was her world, and everyone else was just living in it.

As the crew hustled to get everything in place, Jasmine's poised composure remained. She knew that at the end of the day, it was her image that mattered most, and she would make sure everyone around her understood that.

Chapter 14

The cameras were rolling, and Jasmine strutted toward Trey, exuding all the confidence of a seasoned diva. The final scene of the music video was underway, and Jasmine was determined to make it unforgettable. Her movements were deliberate and perfectly timed, drawing all eyes to her as she moved closer to Trey, who watched her with an amused grin playing on his lips. His gaze softened as she approached, clearly enjoying the show she was putting on.

One of the crew members, still trying to maintain professionalism amidst the chaos of the shoot, stepped forward holding a bottle of water, his voice tentative.

"Jasmine, would you like some water?"

She glanced at the bottle, her face contorting into a brief expression of disdain. To her, it was nothing more than an insignificant prop in the grand scene she was creating. Jasmine let out a small, contemptuous laugh before she waved her hand dismissively, as if the bottle itself had offended her.

"Do I look like I need water? Please," she scoffed, her tone dripping with arrogance. The crew member stood frozen for a moment, unsure whether to take her response seriously or if it was just another display of her overwhelming self-importance. Jasmine brushed past him, every step oozing with self-assurance as she made her way toward Trey, her eyes never leaving him.

The crew, visibly relieved by the brief pause in Jasmine's antics, let out a collective sigh. The tension that had built throughout the shoot seemed to melt away, but it was clear they were all just trying to get through it without further incident.

Trey, however, was not bothered by her antics in the slightest. Instead, he grinned broadly, watching her approach with a mix of admiration and amusement. As Jasmine reached him, she shot him a playful look, as though daring him to react to her domineering presence.

"You really know how to steal a scene," he remarked, his grin widening.

Jasmine, not missing a beat, returned his look with equal smugness, her voice dripping with pride. "I didn't come here to blend in, Trey. I came to own it."

Her words hung in the air, a testament to the self-confidence she had cultivated over the years. Trey chuckled, clearly entertained by her boldness. The moment was electric, both of them fully aware of the underlying tension that had built between them.

As the director called out, "Cut!" signaling the end of the shoot, Jasmine's eyes lingered on Trey for a moment longer. She gave him a knowing smile, almost as if they were sharing an unspoken agreement that the day had been hers and she had certainly made it one to remember.

The room is quiet except for the low hum of the screen, where the recently finished music video plays, showcasing Jasmine's every move. Trey sits back in his lavish office chair, his posture relaxed but his attention focused entirely on the woman in his lap. Jasmine is perched gracefully, her back straight, her body pressing lightly against him. The dim light from the screen flickers across her face, making her look even more radiant.

She watches herself on the video, her eyes gleaming with satisfaction. Every move, every step—she had executed them all flawlessly. The music pulses through the air as she sways to the rhythm, as if she could feel the beat inside her bones.

Trey's hand moves subtly to her waist, his fingers brushing against her skin as he leans in, his lips almost touching her ear.

"You've got some serious moves, Jasmine," he whispers, his voice low and smooth, "You were the star of that video."

Jasmine's lips curl into a confident smile at his praise. She leans back slightly, flicking her hair over her shoulder and tilting her head toward the screen with a proud, almost smug expression. Her eyes never leave the video as she watches herself with a sense of ownership.

"I know," she replies coolly, her voice dripping with arrogance. "I wasn't about to let anyone else shine."

Her words hang in the air, filled with the self-assurance that she's become known for. The video, in her mind, was more than just a piece of work—it was a showcase of her talent, her magnetism. She wasn't just performing; she was owning every moment of it.

Behind them, standing off to the side in the shadow of the room, the director watches intently, his arms crossed. His expression is tight, his face set in a frown. It's clear he doesn't share Trey's enthusiasm for Jasmine's performance. His eyes flicker toward her occasionally, but he's careful not to engage. His disapproval is palpable, yet he doesn't voice it, choosing instead to remain silent, waiting for the moment to pass.

Jasmine's phone suddenly vibrates on the table, interrupting the moment. The noise breaks the tension in the room, and she glances at the screen, her frown deepening when she sees the caller ID: Sarah.

With a sigh, she slides off Trey's lap and stands up, smoothing out her outfit as she does. Her expression shifts slightly, no longer the smug diva from moments ago.

"I'll be right back," Jasmine mutters, almost under her breath. She grabs her phone off the table with one swift motion, a flicker of irritation crossing her face as she glances at the screen again. Without another word, she turns and heads out of the office, leaving Trey in his chair and the director standing quietly in the background.

Trey watches her go, raising an eyebrow. There's a trace of curiosity in his gaze, but he doesn't make any attempt to stop her. He leans back, propping his feet up on the desk, waiting to see what happens next. He doesn't seem concerned, but the flicker of interest in his eyes suggests that Jasmine's next move might not be as predictable as he had hoped.

The director, however, doesn't share his calm demeanor. He shoots a glance at Trey, his disapproving expression barely concealed, but remains silent. The tension between them lingers, unspoken. The director knows something that Trey doesn't—that Jasmine's presence on set wasn't as seamless as it appeared. But for now, he too stays quiet, awaiting Jasmine's return, whatever that might bring.

Sarah said with a smile, "Hey! I just wanted to check in. I'm at my mom's place—she's treating me really well. I was worried after everything, but she's been super kind."

Jasmine rolled her eyes, her fingers tapping impatiently on the cold wall of the hallway as she leaned against it. The silence in the hallway felt suffocating, the faint hum of voices in the distance the only noise breaking the stillness. "That's great, Sarah. I'm really happy for you. You know, everything's just... fine here. Super busy, as usual. But hey, how are you really doing?" she replied, her voice softening a little but still laced with an edge of tension.

"Oh, you know," Sarah continued, "I'm actually doing okay. Better than I thought. Honestly, I was worried at first—after everything went down with, you know, him... but my mom's been really sweet. I think she missed me. She's been taking care of me like I'm still her little girl."

Jasmine sighed, pushing herself off the wall and pacing the hallway. She felt the weight of the day pressing on her, her steps quick and deliberate as her hand brushed the cold stone of the grand staircase's railing. "Well, that's... lovely, Sarah. I'm sure it's exactly what you needed. A little TLC from mom after all the mess. Good for you. Really," she said, her tone laced with sarcasm, though a flicker of something softer lingered behind the words.

Sarah said with a smile, her voice warm and filled with concern.

"Hey, I just wanted to check in. I'm at my mom's place—she's treating me really well. I was worried after everything, but she's been super kind."

Jasmine rolled her eyes, her lips curling into a thin, dismissive line as she leans against the cold hallway wall. Her tone is dry, almost biting as she responds, clearly uninterested in the niceties of Sarah's world.

"That's good, I guess," she said, her voice flat, "but don't let her drag you into all that religious nonsense, okay?"

Sarah's voice faltered slightly, sensing the sharp edge in Jasmine's words. She hesitated for a moment before responding, trying to keep the conversation light.

"Well, it's not exactly like that," she said carefully, "she's just been trying to help me sort through everything, you know? I don't really believe in all of it either, but it's helping me clear my head."

Jasmine's laugh is short and humorless. She straightens up, crossing her arms, her eyes glinting with something between irritation and indifference.

"Yeah, sure," Jasmine said, her voice laced with sarcasm. "Whatever helps you sleep at night. But don't get too cozy with that whole 'finding your purpose' crap. People like her suck you in with their preachy nonsense, and you end up stuck in some fantasy world where everything's a miracle. Trust me, I've seen it all before."

Sarah's words came out softer this time, a little unsure, though still filled with the desire to maintain some connection.

"I'm not saying I'm going to become someone else, Jasmine. I'm just... I just need a little peace. And I don't think it's that bad. She's been there for me when I needed it, and that's all I'm asking for right now."

Jasmine snorted, her eyes rolling in exasperation as she shifted her weight from one foot to the other. Her voice was scornful, as if Sarah were nothing more than a naïve child who still believed in fairy tales.

"Peace?" she said, the words dripping with contempt. "Don't kid yourself. You're just trying to fill the void with some feel-good bullshit. It never works out in the end. People like her, with all their fake kindness and 'life lessons,' they'll have you wrapped around their little finger before you even realize it."

The silence stretched between them as Sarah let out a soft sigh. She tried to find a way to keep things from unraveling, but it was clear Jasmine wasn't in the mood for any of it.

"Jasmine, I'm not asking you to understand. I just want you to know that I'm okay. You don't have to keep pushing me away.

I'm not trying to change, I just... I'm trying to find my way through all the chaos."

Jasmine's jaw tightened, her eyes narrowing as she glared at the floor. She wasn't about to let anyone—especially Sarah—get under her skin. Her tone was sharp, cutting, and final.

"Find your way all you want. But don't expect me to care. I've had my fill of people like you. And honestly, if you think all this crap is going to fix you, you're just setting yourself up for disappointment."

There was a long, drawn-out pause. Sarah's voice quivered, but she tried to hold her ground.

"I'm not expecting anything from you, Jasmine," she said softly. "But I need to do this for myself."

Jasmine's face hardened further, her lips curling into a snarl. She could feel the walls she'd built around herself getting thicker, stronger. There was no room for weakness, no room for understanding. Not now. Not ever.

"Fine," Jasmine said, her voice cold and dismissive. "Do whatever you want. But don't come running to me when it all falls apart. I'm done playing the 'good friend' who listens to all this nonsense."

Before Sarah could reply, Jasmine cut her off, the tone of finality unmistakable.

"I've got better things to do than listen to you whine about your 'new life.' Catch you later."

Without waiting for a response, Jasmine ended the call, tossing her phone onto the nearby table with a hard thud. She stood there for a moment, breathing heavily, her mind already moving on to the next thing.

she slammed the phone down onto the table, the clack of it echoing through the empty hallway. The moment the call ended, a sense of satisfaction washed over her. No more strings to tie her down, no more fake connections.

Jasmine shook her head, rolling her eyes as if the whole situation was beneath her. She could already feel the frustration simmering beneath the surface, but she pushed it down with practiced ease.

What a waste of time, she thought, her lips curling into a smug, self-satisfied smile as she turned away from the hallway, her heels clicking loudly against the floor as she strode off.

The cold, unfeeling part of her took over, and she pushed the fleeting feeling of guilt aside. There was no room for weakness, no room for regret. As she walked away, a part of her felt free in the certainty that she had nothing left to hold her back.

She didn't need anyone. Not Sarah. Not anyone.

Jasmine slipped into the office, her heels clicking softly on the polished marble floor. The room was dim, lit only by the glow of the desk lamp and the faint city lights creeping through the large windows. As she approached the desk, she casually slipped her phone into her bag, her mind on a dozen other things. She hadn't expected to be back here so late, but there were always last-minute things to attend to in this business.

The faint hum of the city's nightlife seemed to seep into the office, adding a surreal ambiance to the otherwise quiet space. The leather chairs, dark wood desk, and the minimalist art on the walls gave the room an air of professionalism, but the heavy scent of cigarette smoke told another story. Trey, who usually seemed composed and in control, was leaning back in his chair, his arms crossed, a look of detached amusement on his face as he stared across the desk. His gaze wasn't on her, though. His focus was solely on the figure sitting across from him.

Jasmine froze mid-step. Her breath hitched as she took in the man sitting opposite Trey. He was a stark contrast to the usual visitors that came and went from this office, and for a moment, she felt a cold shiver run down her spine. The man was dressed in an oversized hoodie, its dark fabric almost swallowing his frame, with a leather jacket that looked like it had seen better days. His face was rough, unshaven, with patches of stubble that gave him a worn-down look, like he hadn't bothered to take care of himself in days—or perhaps weeks. His eyes were bloodshot, glazed over, as though he hadn't slept in a long while, and his expression was one of quiet but intense focus, like someone who knew exactly what they were doing and didn't need to explain himself to anyone.

A faint cloud of smoke curled lazily in the air around him. He took a drag from a half-burnt cigarette, flicking ash into a small, nearly overflowing ashtray on the desk. The smoke seemed to add to the heavy atmosphere of the room, making it feel almost suffocating. Jasmine's gaze dropped to the desk, and her heart skipped a beat. There, between them, was a small black duffel bag, unzipped slightly. The contents were partially visible, and her stomach lurched as she saw the stacks of cash. The kind of money that didn't come from legitimate sources. The kind of money that made the hair on the back of her neck stand up.

The office felt smaller now, the air thicker. The walls, once just a backdrop to business meetings, now seemed to close in around her, enclosing her in a room that suddenly felt like a trap.

Jasmine's first instinct was to turn around and leave, to walk away and pretend she hadn't seen any of this. But the look on Trey's face stopped her in her tracks. He didn't seem surprised by her presence, and the way he was leaning back in his chair—too relaxed, too at ease—told her everything she needed to know. This was something normal for him, something he was used to. Something she wasn't used to. His eyes met hers briefly, giving her a look that was more a warning than anything else.

The message was clear: Don't interrupt. Stay out of it.

Jasmine swallowed hard, her fingers tightening around the strap of her bag. Her eyes flicked between Trey and the man across the desk. The room felt suddenly colder, as if the very air had shifted. She took a hesitant step back, but she knew she couldn't just walk away. Not now. Not with the tension in the room so thick, so palpable.

The man across from Trey didn't even glance at her. He was too absorbed in his conversation with Trey, his voice a low, gravelly murmur. Jasmine strained to hear what they were saying, but the words were muffled, drowned out by the hum of her own thoughts. She stood there for a moment, unsure of what to do. Should she stay and pretend she hadn't seen anything? Should she walk out and risk making things worse?

Trey didn't give her any indication of what he expected. His eyes were focused solely on the man before him, his expression unreadable. Jasmine knew he wasn't the type to engage in small talk when something serious was going down. And this, she realized, was serious.

She took another cautious step forward, trying to force herself to act like she belonged here. As much as she wanted to ignore it all, as much as she wanted to walk away from this uncomfortable situation, she couldn't help herself. The curiosity was eating at her, gnawing away at her every moment. What was going on here? What were they discussing? And why was there so much money involved?

Jasmine crossed her arms, trying to appear calm, collected, but inside, her mind was racing. Her gaze kept flicking back to the duffel bag, the stacks of cash—money she knew didn't come from anything legal. The world she lived in wasn't one where the rules were always followed. She'd seen enough to understand how things worked, how people in this business operated, but this? This was something else entirely. This wasn't just shady—it was downright dangerous.

Trey's voice finally broke through her thoughts. He spoke low, his tone smooth and casual, as if they were discussing nothing more than a simple business transaction. But the words—if she could catch even a fraction of them—spoke volumes.

"You know how it works," Trey said, his voice laced with authority. "You give me the cash, I take care of the rest. You've been asking for a while, and now you've got it. But you need to understand, this doesn't come without strings attached."

Jasmine's heart skipped a beat. What the hell were they talking about? Who was the man across from Trey, and what kind of deal were they striking?

The man, still silent, nodded slowly. His rough fingers tapped against the edge of the duffel bag, as if contemplating something. Then, in a raspy voice, he finally spoke.

"You think I don't know the game?" His words were like gravel, each syllable thick with suspicion and bitterness. "You're offering protection, Trey. But you don't fool me. I've seen how this works. Protection doesn't come free."

Trey leaned forward slightly, his eyes narrowing just enough to show he wasn't impressed by the man's bravado.

"I'm not in the business of charity," Trey said, his voice cold. "But you know that. If you want to stay alive in this town, you'll pay the price. You don't get to pick and choose. That's not how it works."

Jasmine's stomach tightened. Protection? What kind of protection were they talking about? Was this about the kind of protection that could only be bought with dirty money? Or was there something even darker going on here, something she wasn't privy to?

The man grunted, flicking ash off his cigarette into the tray. His hands trembled slightly, the only sign of his nervousness. He leaned back in his chair, his eyes meeting Trey's with a mixture of defiance and acceptance.

"Yeah, I know how this goes," the man muttered. "But don't think for a second I'm gonna trust you. I've seen your type before. I know how this ends."

Trey didn't flinch. His eyes stayed fixed on the man, unreadable, as always.

"You don't have to trust me," Trey replied, his voice steady. "You just have to pay up and stay out of my way. That's all. Simple as that."

Jasmine's mind was racing, trying to piece together what she was hearing. Was this some sort of underworld deal? Were they discussing protection money? Was Trey involved in something far more dangerous than she ever imagined?

The man sat in silence for a moment, contemplating Trey's words. Then, with a grunt, he reached into his jacket and pulled out an envelope. He slid it across the desk with a grim smile.

"Consider it done," he said.

Trey didn't move to take the envelope right away. Instead, he simply nodded, his expression unreadable.

"Good," he said, before adding, "You've made the right choice. Just remember—things won't be so easy from here on out."

The man gave him a half-smile, one that didn't quite reach his eyes. He stubbed out his cigarette and stood up, grabbing the duffel bag and tossing it over his shoulder.

"I'll remember," he said. "And I'll be back when the time comes."

Jasmine stood frozen in the doorway, watching as the man turned and left the office. The weight of the conversation hung in the air long after the door had clicked shut behind him. Trey didn't say a word, but Jasmine could feel the tension still thick in the room.

She didn't know what to think anymore. What had she just witnessed? And what did it mean for her?

Trey leaned back in his chair, his eyes drifting to her finally. There was a flicker of something in his gaze—something unreadable, but heavy.

"You should go home, Jasmine," he said, his tone cool, detached. "Nothing for you here tonight."

Jasmine stood there, unable to move. Her mind was reeling, too many questions left unanswered. But one thing was certain: Trey was deep into something far darker than she had ever realized, and now she was caught in the middle of it.

She didn't know what to do or where to go from here. But as she turned to leave, she knew that nothing would ever be the same again.

Chapter 15

Jasmine stood frozen in the doorway, her breath caught in her throat. The office was suddenly thick with tension, and every sense she had screamed that something dangerous was unfolding in front of her. Her fingers tightened around her bag strap, unsure if she should stay or leave. The man across from Trey didn't even look up at her as he sifted through the cash on the desk, his rough hands quickly flicking through the bills like he was familiar with the process—like he had done this a thousand times before.

The room was heavy with the smell of cigarette smoke, the haze swirling around in lazy spirals as Trey leaned back in his chair, his eyes half-lidded, taking in the whole scene with a detached calmness. His expression was a mask, as it always was. There was no panic, no urgency in the way he sat there—just that cool, unwavering confidence that made him look like he was in control of everything. As always.

The man across from him, however, wasn't nearly as relaxed. His eyes, bloodshot and wild, darted between the stacks of bills and Trey. He was gruff and impatient, his hands rough as they tugged at the bills, almost as if he didn't trust that the money was real.

"This'll cover the last drop," the man grunted, his voice deep and raspy. "But you know I ain't fronting the next one without the full amount upfront, Trey."

His words hung in the air like an ultimatum, the weight of his statement pressing down on the room. Jasmine felt the pulse of it. The man wasn't playing around. This wasn't just a casual transaction—it was serious, and she had no doubt that if things went wrong, it would spiral out of control quickly.

Trey, unfazed, took another drag from his cigarette, exhaling a cloud of smoke slowly as he leaned back in his chair. His posture was casual, but there was something dangerous in the way he kept his eyes fixed on the man across from him.

"You'll get your money," Trey said, his voice cool and steady, almost rehearsed. "The next shipment's bigger, so no worries. Business is good, man."

His words were meant to reassure, but the air was thick with the tension that neither of them could deny. Trey wasn't a fool— he knew this deal was risky, but he had a way of making everything sound smooth, no matter how rocky it really was. The man grunted in response, clearly not interested in small talk. He leaned forward slightly, his eyes narrowing as he spoke again, his voice dropping even lower.

"You better hope so," the man said, his tone turning more serious, more urgent. "Cops have been sniffing around, and I'm not looking to get burned 'cause your operation's too loud."

The words struck Jasmine like a slap to the face. Cops. Sniffing around. She didn't know much about Trey's business—she had never asked and had never wanted to know—but this… this was something she had never imagined. Her stomach turned as she realized the full scope of what she had walked into. She had been naive, thinking that the late nights, the shady deals, and the business talk that was always veiled in secrecy were just part of the job. But this? This was something much deeper, much more dangerous.

She instinctively took a step back, hoping the man wouldn't notice her standing there, but her movement caught his eye. For the briefest moment, his gaze flickered over to her. It was a cold, calculating glance, the kind of look that made her feel like she was being weighed and measured, judged by someone who had seen too much of the world to care about anyone who didn't matter. His eyes were sharp, bloodshot, and calculating, like a predator sizing up its prey. He didn't say anything, but the glance was enough. He knew she was there, and he didn't care.

Jasmine's heart pounded in her chest. She shouldn't be here. She shouldn't be witnessing any of this. But she was, and she couldn't seem to turn away. There was a part of her, deep inside, that was terrified of what this meant for her. Her life, her choices, everything she thought she knew about Trey—it was all coming undone in this single, tense moment. The man across from Trey was dangerous, that much was clear. And Trey himself, despite his calm demeanor, was too involved in something dark for her to even begin to understand.

Trey, however, seemed unfazed by the man's words. He exhaled another puff of smoke, his gaze never wavering from the man across from him.

"Don't worry about it," Trey said, his voice smooth and unwavering. "We're all set. If the cops are sniffing around, they'll get distracted. They always do. And you know the next shipment will go off without a hitch."

The man didn't look convinced, but he didn't argue further. He grunted again, pushing the duffel bag closer to Trey. The sound of the zipper being pulled up echoed in the otherwise silent room.

"I'll be back for the next one," the man said, his voice gruff. "You better not be playing me, Trey. If this goes south, I'll make sure you regret it."

Trey simply nodded, his eyes hardening slightly. The man was still a loose cannon, unpredictable, but Trey had a way of handling people like him. His eyes never left the man's face as he slowly slid the duffel bag toward him, the cash inside now safely hidden from view.

"You'll get what you're owed," Trey said, his voice firm, but there was an underlying tension in his words. "Now get out of here. We'll talk when the next shipment is ready."

The man stood up, grabbing the duffel bag with one hand, the cigarette still burning in his other. He took one last glance at Trey before turning toward the door, not sparing a second look toward

Jasmine. He wasn't concerned with her. She was just another part of the scenery, something in the background.

Jasmine, however, couldn't tear her eyes away from the man as he walked out. The door clicked shut behind him, but the weight of what had just happened still lingered in the room, thick and suffocating. Trey sat back in his chair, his eyes still on the door, his fingers tapping idly on the armrest.

Jasmine stayed frozen for a moment longer, her heart still racing, her mind struggling to process everything. She didn't know what to say, didn't know what to do. She had just witnessed something she never should have seen. Something dangerous. And now, she was stuck in the middle of it.

Trey didn't acknowledge her presence right away. He didn't need to. He knew she was there, and he knew she had heard everything. Finally, after what felt like an eternity, he leaned forward, his eyes meeting hers with that same unreadable calm.

"You're still here?" Trey asked, his voice low, but there was an edge to it now, something sharp that made Jasmine's breath catch. "I told you to stay out of this, Jasmine."

She didn't respond right away. How could she? There was too much going through her mind. Too many questions she didn't have answers to. The room seemed smaller now, the walls pressing in, and the air felt heavy with the weight of everything that had just unfolded.

"You're in over your head," Trey continued, his voice softer now, but no less serious. "You don't know what you just walked into. And you sure as hell don't want to know."

Jasmine opened her mouth to say something, but the words stuck in her throat. She didn't know what she was supposed to say. The man had just walked in with a duffel bag full of cash, talking about cops and shipments and things she didn't understand. And Trey—Trey was involved.

She could feel her stomach churn with a mixture of fear and disbelief. This wasn't the man she had known. This wasn't the guy she had been working with. Trey was a lot more than just a businessman, and Jasmine was starting to realize she had stepped into a world she wasn't prepared for.

"I can't just walk away from this," Jasmine finally said, her voice barely a whisper. Her words felt weak, uncertain, but they were all she had.

Trey didn't respond immediately. He just stared at her, his expression unreadable.

"You don't have a choice," he said finally. "You're already too deep. So, you can either stay and keep your mouth shut, or you can leave. But don't think it's that simple."

Jasmine's heart pounded in her chest as she processed his words. She was already in too deep. But what did that mean for her?

Jasmine's breath caught in her throat as the mention of cops hit her like a thunderclap. Her mind raced, the words echoing in her ears as the weight of the situation settled over her like a suffocating fog. Cops. Sniffing around. The pieces clicked together, and she suddenly understood just how deep she had gotten into something far darker than she'd ever imagined. The world she had thought she knew—business, deals, money—was all just a veneer, a distraction from something far more dangerous.

Her body moved on instinct. Without even thinking, she took a small, hasty step back toward the door, her eyes wide with panic. Every nerve in her body screamed at her to leave, to escape whatever this was before it all came crashing down. Her fingers brushed the door handle, but the sharpness in Trey's gaze froze her in her tracks.

Trey's eyes locked onto hers, his warning look now colder, harder, more intense. It wasn't just a casual glance—this was a silent command, an unspoken message that she wasn't going anywhere without consequences.

"Don't even think about it," Trey's voice cut through the thick silence, sharp as a blade. It was low, controlled, but the underlying edge of danger was unmistakable. Jasmine's pulse quickened as she felt the weight of his words press down on her, forcing her to stay rooted in place.

The room felt smaller now, as if the walls were closing in around her. The air, thick with the stale smell of cigarettes and the lingering tension, made it hard to breathe. Jasmine swallowed hard, trying to steady her shaking hands. Her mind screamed at her to run, to get out while she still had the chance. But something about Trey's presence, the way he commanded the room, made it impossible to move.

Jasmine shifted her weight from one foot to the other, her eyes darting to the door and back to Trey. The man who had just left was still fresh in her mind, his rough features, the way he had talked about cops and shipments. She hadn't imagined it; this was real. This was something far beyond her understanding, something dangerous.

"You don't get it, do you?" Trey's voice pulled her from her thoughts, and she looked up to find him leaning forward, his elbows on the desk, his gaze unblinking, piercing right through her. "This isn't a game. You're in deeper than you think. And there's no easy way out."

Jasmine opened her mouth to say something, anything, but the words felt hollow in her throat. She could feel the heavy pressure of his stare, the weight of his expectations, and the overwhelming sense that she had already stepped too far into this world to back out now. The realization hit her hard, like a punch to the gut—she wasn't just an observer. She was part of this now, whether she liked it or not.

Trey sat back in his chair, the cool, confident air around him not faltering for a second. He took a long drag from his cigarette, the ember glowing bright in the dim light, and slowly exhaled, watching the smoke curl in lazy spirals around him.

"You think this is about money?" His voice was almost a whisper now, but it carried a weight of authority that made

Jasmine's stomach twist. "It's not. This is about survival. You get too close, you get burned."

Jasmine's chest tightened as the reality of his words hit her. She was standing on the edge of something far more dangerous than she had ever imagined. She had always thought Trey was a businessman, someone who knew how to make money, someone who could be trusted. But this? This was a different side of him entirely, one she had never seen and now couldn't ignore.

The man who had just left had been rough, unpredictable, but Trey? Trey was calculating. Every word he spoke, every glance he gave, was carefully chosen, carefully measured. He wasn't just running a business—he was running an operation, a world that Jasmine had never even known existed.

"You're part of this now," Trey continued, his voice still calm, but there was a flicker of something dark in his eyes. "And you'll stay part of it. You either keep your head down and don't ask questions, or you get the hell out and pretend you never saw any of this. But don't think for a second that you can walk away without consequences."

Jasmine felt the weight of his words settle deep into her bones. Her chest tightened, and she found herself holding her breath, as if the very act of breathing would make everything more real. She had no idea what Trey was capable of, but standing here, feeling the pressure of his gaze, she knew she didn't want to find out. Not now. Not ever.

Her mind raced, the door just a few feet away, and yet she felt like she was trapped in a room with no exits. She could leave, but what would happen then? Would she walk away from all of this, only to find herself caught in a web she couldn't escape? Would Trey find a way to pull her back in?

Or worse, would he let her leave, only to have someone else track her down later, to make sure she never spoke a word of what she had seen?

The door. She needed to get to the door. But she couldn't move. She was paralyzed by fear, by the reality of the situation. Trey's eyes never left hers as he waited, as if he were waiting for her to decide her fate, to make her move.

"You don't want to make the wrong choice, Jasmine," Trey said quietly, his voice almost gentle now, but it was a false kindness. It was the calm before the storm. "Once you step in, there's no turning back. Not for you. Not for anyone."

Jasmine opened her mouth, but the words caught in her throat. She didn't know what to say, didn't know how to answer. She had been naive, had thought she could play along, stay in the background. But the game had changed. Trey was no longer just a business partner, no longer someone she could trust. He was something else now—something dangerous, something she couldn't understand.

Her heart pounded as the silence stretched between them, thick and suffocating. Trey's gaze never wavered, and Jasmine couldn't look away, her mind still reeling, her body frozen in place.

"You're stuck with me, Jasmine," Trey said finally, his voice a low murmur, almost like a promise. "And you'll learn to deal with it. Or you won't. But make no mistake—you're in this now. There's no getting out."

The words hit her like a wave, crashing over her with a force that left her breathless. She had stepped into a world of shadows, of power plays and danger, and there was no going back. She didn't know if she was ready for this world, but one thing was clear: her life would never be the same again.

And as the weight of his words settled in, Jasmine realized something that terrified her more than anything else: Trey was right. She was already in too deep.

The tension in the room is thick as the man finishes securing the duffel bag. He grunts lowly, a sound that sends a chill through the otherwise still air. As he closes the zipper on the bag, his rough fingers brush over the stacks of cash inside, making the money seem almost too heavy for him to handle. His eyes flicker to the man sitting across from him, whose expression remains as cool as ever.

"I'm not asking for much," the man growls, his voice tinged with the slightest trace of threat. "Just don't screw me over, alright? You know what happens if things go sideways."

The words hang in the air like a warning. It's clear he's not making an idle threat, and the weight of it is heavy enough to make the whole room feel smaller. The silence stretches as the man waits for a response. His gaze lingers on Trey, looking for any sign of weakness, any crack in the calm façade.

Trey, unbothered, flicks the last bit of ash from his cigarette with a lazy flick of his fingers. His eyes lock with the man's—steady, unwavering. He's not afraid. He doesn't need to be reminded of the consequences.

"I don't need reminding," Trey says, his voice low and serious. The words are measured, calm, but the underlying menace is clear. He's not someone to be crossed.

The man seems to sense this, his expression darkening slightly as he slings the duffel bag over his shoulder. The weight of the money doesn't seem to phase him; it's as though he's done this a hundred times before. The exchange is over, and it's time for him to leave.

As he stands, his eyes sweep over Jasmine, who remains frozen against the wall. His gaze lingers for a moment longer than necessary, a smirk tugging at the corner of his lips. It's a look that's almost predatory, sizing her up, though he doesn't say anything. He doesn't need to. The smirk says it all.

Chapter 16

Jasmine's breath catches in her throat as his eyes meet hers. She can't help the uneasy feeling that creeps up her spine. Her heart beats louder in her chest, the thrum of it making her feel even more exposed. She presses herself further into the wall, trying to make herself as small as possible. She knows she's no part of this deal, but the way he looks at her makes her feel like she's just a pawn in a much bigger game.

The man strides past her, his steps heavy on the floor, and she instinctively steps aside. As he passes, the faint smell of smoke lingers in the air, sharp and acrid. The scent clings to her for a moment, making her feel like she's trapped in a world that doesn't belong to her, a world she never should have gotten involved in.

The door shuts with a soft thud behind him, but Jasmine doesn't move. She remains pressed against the wall, her eyes glued to the space where the man had just stood. Her mind races, replaying the encounter, the tension, the threat.

Her pulse slows as the reality of the situation sinks in. She had never wanted this, never asked for any of it. But now, she's in it— too deep to back out, too tangled in the mess to pretend it's all just a bad dream.

Trey doesn't seem to notice her unease. He remains calm, collected, flicking the ash from his cigarette into the tray on the desk. He doesn't even glance her way as he adjusts himself in his chair, clearly more focused on the business at hand than on the tension that's thick in the air.

Jasmine takes a deep breath, straightening up and shaking her head. She's not sure what to make of this anymore. The world she thought she understood, the world of flashing lights, expensive clothes, and VIP access, suddenly feels shallow, dangerous. She never signed up for this. She never imagined it would go this far. Yet here she is, still standing in the middle of it.

"Everything alright?" Trey's voice breaks the silence, his tone cool, almost too casual. But Jasmine can hear the undercurrent of something else—something that tells her he's been watching her all along.

She looks at him, her expression hardening. "Yeah," she says, the word coming out like it's been forced from her lips. She's not sure if she believes it herself. "Just peachy."

Trey doesn't respond, but the way he eyes her, the way he watches her like he's sizing her up, is enough to make her skin crawl. She knows she's in deeper than she ever wanted to be, and there's no way out now. The stakes have been raised, and she's caught in the middle of it all, whether she likes it or not.

She turns away, taking a few slow steps toward the door, but her mind is still reeling from everything that just happened. She needs to clear her head, but she knows it won't be that easy. Not anymore. She's tangled in this web, and there's no escaping it now.

Jasmine leans back against the cool wall of the hallway, her heart racing. Her mind races even faster, replaying the conversation she just overheard. The door to Trey's office is now closed, but the tension still lingers in the air, thick and suffocating. She can still smell the faint scent of smoke, and it makes her stomach turn.

What had that man meant when he mentioned the cops? Was Trey really involved in something so dangerous? Jasmine tries to shake off the unsettling thoughts that swirl in her head. She was never supposed to be this deep into Trey's world. But somehow, here she is, caught between a dangerous man and a series of choices she never saw coming.

With a shaky breath, she pushes herself off the wall and takes a few steps toward the office door. She pauses just outside, taking a moment to steady herself before stepping back inside. Trey is still seated behind his desk, his posture now much more relaxed. The tension that had been thick in the room just moments ago seems to have dissolved, replaced by an air of calm that unnerves her even more.

A thin stream of smoke curls lazily from his cigarette, twisting in the air like a snake. He leans back in his chair, eyes focused on her as if waiting for her to speak. But his casual demeanor only adds to her unease. There's something cold about the way he's looking at her now, like he's expecting her to fall into line without asking too many questions.

"Who was that?" Trey asks, his voice low and smooth, but there's something about the question that makes it feel like more than just idle curiosity.

Jasmine hesitates for a moment, caught off guard by the question. She was already trying to move past the conversation, but now that he's asking, it's like all of her emotions are flooding to the surface. She was supposed to be someone who could handle this, someone who didn't ask questions or get tangled in things that didn't concern her. But now, it's clear that the line between what's her business and what's not is starting to blur.

She stops herself before answering, suddenly aware of the weight of his words. He isn't asking about her, he's asking about what she's seen, what she's overheard. He's trying to gauge whether she's truly in the dark, or if she's starting to put the pieces together.

Jasmine waves her hand dismissively, trying to brush off the question before it can drag her deeper into something she's already regretting. "No one important. Just a friend checking in." Her words sound rehearsed, too smooth, as if she's trying to convince herself more than him. But she knows Trey can see right through her. He always does.

Trey doesn't press the issue, but the way he watches her as she speaks tells Jasmine everything she needs to know. He knows something's off, and he's waiting for her to slip up. It's only a matter of time before she does.

Without saying anything else, Trey leans forward in his chair, his hand reaching for her. She feels a sudden pull, like he's drawing her in, commanding her presence with just the smallest of gestures. Jasmine doesn't resist as he pulls her back onto his lap, her body sinking into his, feeling the warmth of his touch against her skin. She sighs, trying to ease the tension that's still knotted tight in her chest. But she can't ignore the feeling gnawing at her insides.

"Do you have something to say?" Trey asks, his voice quieter now, like he's sensing her hesitation.

Jasmine shakes her head, trying to force a smile, but it feels brittle, like it might break at any second. "You know I always agree with you, my love," she says smoothly, wrapping an arm around his shoulders. Her fingers trail lightly along the curve of his neck, the motion slow, almost absentminded. She tries to focus on the feel of him beneath her, the warmth of his body, the safety in his embrace.

But the smile fades from her lips as her gaze shifts away, her thoughts once again consumed by the conversation she had overheard. She forces herself not to dwell on it, but the more she tries to ignore it, the more the nagging feeling grows.

Trey doesn't notice the change in her expression, or if he does, he doesn't let on. His hand rests on her waist, his fingers tracing small circles on her skin. It's soothing in a way, but the more she feels him, the more it all seems wrong. The words of the suspicious man echo in her mind. The cops. The threats. The money. She wonders just how deep Trey is in this world, and whether she's in over her head.

She swallows hard, shaking her head to clear the thoughts clouding her mind. She can't afford to get caught up in this mess. She knows she should leave, cut ties with Trey, walk away before things get any worse. But she can't bring herself to do it. Part of her wants to believe that it's all a misunderstanding, that Trey is just involved in something small, something temporary. But the more she sees, the more she realizes that she's only fooling herself.

Trey leans in closer, his lips brushing against her neck as he pulls her even tighter against him. His presence is overwhelming, intoxicating, but it's not enough to drown out the doubts creeping into her mind. She forces a laugh, even though it doesn't reach her eyes.

"I'm fine, Trey," she says, her voice softer than she intended. "Everything's fine."

But deep down, she knows it isn't. And no matter how much she tries to convince herself otherwise, she can feel herself slipping deeper into a world that isn't her own—a world of danger, secrets, and lies. And there's no way out now.

Trey tilts his head back, exhaling a cloud of smoke that seems to linger in the air, thick and oppressive. His eyes flicker briefly to Jasmine before narrowing with a mix of impatience and amusement. He runs a hand through his hair, trying to seem casual, but the weight of his expectations presses down on both of them. The silence that follows is heavy, but it's clear he's not about to let it drag on for too long.

"I'm going to see you tonight, right?" His voice cuts through the stillness, smooth but with an edge that makes it sound more like a demand than a question.

Jasmine pauses, her fingers tightening around the edge of the chair, just enough to steady herself. She wasn't ready for this. She hadn't fully processed the conversation she overheard, and now she was stuck here, locked in Trey's world, pretending everything was fine. But it was all slipping away from her, unraveling little by little, and the more she tried to keep it together, the more it felt like the ground beneath her feet was crumbling.

She turns back to face him, trying to suppress the unease creeping up her spine. She forces her lips into a smile, but it feels stiff, fake. It's not the kind of smile that reaches her eyes, the kind that makes her feel like she's truly in control. This one is thin, shallow, and she knows it.

"Yeah, sure," she says, her voice sounding far more uncertain than she'd like. She's trying to keep it together, trying to sound like she's on the same page, but it's getting harder to lie to him. "I'll be there."

Trey doesn't seem convinced, but he doesn't press her further. He watches her for a moment, his gaze calculating, as if weighing her words. The pause stretches out, just long enough for Jasmine to feel her pulse quicken. But then, with a shrug, he dismisses her response, leaning back in his chair once more.

"You should move in already," Trey says casually, taking another drag from his cigarette. "What are you waiting for?"

The words hit her like a cold gust of wind, sharp and unexpected. He had been hinting at this for a while, but hearing it so directly makes her feel cornered, trapped. Jasmine's heart skips a beat as her stomach churns uncomfortably. She hadn't prepared herself for this. She had been stalling, hoping to delay the inevitable, but now it seems like Trey is no longer willing to wait.

"You know how my mother is…" Jasmine begins, her voice faltering slightly. She can feel the tension in the room, the pressure building as she tries to buy herself more time. "Just give me a little more time to convince her."

Trey rolls his eyes, a dismissive gesture that makes her stomach tighten further. He takes another slow drag from his cigarette, his expression one of frustration. It's not just impatience, though—it's something deeper, something more possessive. Jasmine can feel the weight of his expectations, and she knows she's walking a fine line here. But she's not ready to make the leap yet, not yet.

"You've been saying that for weeks," Trey mutters, his tone dripping with irritation. "What's the hold-up? You're not some little girl anymore. You should be making your own decisions."

Jasmine bites the inside of her cheek, trying to keep her composure. She doesn't want to argue. She doesn't want to make him angry, especially when she's already feeling like everything is slipping out of her control. But the words cut deeper than they should. They remind her of the situation she's trying to avoid, the life she's trying to hold onto. But that life is slowly being pulled away, piece by piece.

"You don't get it," she says, her voice quieter now, but still firm. "It's not that easy. She's... she's my mother, Trey. It's complicated."

Trey scoffs, the sound dismissive and sharp. "Complicated? You're an adult now. You don't need her permission to live your life."

His words sting, but Jasmine knows he doesn't understand. He doesn't know what it's like to live under the thumb of someone who always has an opinion about your choices, someone who holds your every move over your head like a shadow. She tries not to let it show, but it's hard not to feel that familiar weight pressing down on her chest.

"I'll figure it out," Jasmine says, trying to sound more certain than she feels. "I just need a little more time. I promise."

Trey exhales slowly, his expression unreadable as he stares at her. He doesn't say anything right away, but Jasmine can feel his eyes on her, sharp and calculating. The silence stretches between them, thick and uncomfortable, and for a moment, Jasmine wonders if he's losing patience with her, wondering if she's truly worth the trouble.

Finally, Trey takes one last drag from his cigarette before flicking the ash into the tray. He leans forward slightly, his gaze softening just a little, but there's still an underlying tension in his posture.

"I'm not going to wait forever," he says, his voice quieter now, but no less intense. "You know what I want, Jasmine. And if you can't give me that…" He lets the sentence hang in the air, unfinished, but the implication is clear.

Jasmine nods quickly, trying to keep the panic at bay. "I know. I'll handle it. I promise."

Trey doesn't say anything more, but the way he looks at her makes her feel like there's more riding on this than she's prepared for. She can see the doubt in his eyes, but there's something else there too—something she doesn't want to acknowledge. He's used to getting what he wants, and if she doesn't come through for him, she knows it won't end well.

With a final, lingering look, Trey gets to his feet, his movements slow and deliberate. He gives her a small, almost imperceptible smile, but it doesn't reach his eyes.

"I'll see you tonight," he says simply, before turning and walking toward the door.

Jasmine watches him leave, the sound of his footsteps fading as the door shuts behind him. She's left standing there, feeling like the walls are closing in around her. The weight of everything— the promises, the lies, the choices—feels heavier than ever.

She's caught in the middle of a life she never expected, surrounded by people who want things from her that she's not sure she can give. And as much as she tries to convince herself she's in control, she knows deep down that things are about to get much, much harder.

Chapter 17

The living room is bathed in warm sunlight that filters through the curtains, casting a soft glow over the space. On the couch, two women sit, an open Bible resting on the coffee table between them. Their conversation is quiet, but it's filled with the weight of a spiritual awakening.

One of them speaks softly, her voice tender but filled with new understanding.

"I've been thinking a lot about what you've shared, especially about Jesus... and salvation," she says.

The other woman, with a gentle and loving smile, looks at her, her eyes reflecting both compassion and the deep hope she has for this journey.

"It's never too late to come to Him," she says, her voice filled with warmth. "He's always waiting, arms wide open, ready to welcome you."

The first woman's eyes glisten, a wave of emotion catching her off guard. She glances down at her hands, as if steadying herself, gathering the courage to voice what has been stirring in her heart for so long.

"I think… I think I'm ready. I want to receive Jesus," she says quietly.

The second woman's face lights up with joy. She clasps her hands together in gratitude and happiness, beaming with excitement for this new chapter that is about to begin.

"Oh, that's such a beautiful decision," she says, her voice filled with joy. "I'm so happy for you."

The first woman feels her heart race with both excitement and relief. She had been searching for something beyond herself, something to fill the emptiness that always seemed to linger. Now, she could feel it—like she was stepping into something greater than what she had imagined. The other woman's words make it all the more real, like she had found the missing piece of her life.

"I'm scared… but I know it's right," she whispers, feeling vulnerable but certain.

"Fear is normal," the second woman reassures her. "But trust me when I say that this decision will change everything. It's like stepping out of the darkness into the light. You're not alone, and Jesus will walk with you every step of the way."

The first woman feels a warmth rise from within her as the reassurance settles in. She wasn't just making a decision; she was beginning a new chapter in her life. The words "you're not alone" resonate deeply, bringing an unexpected sense of peace to her heart.

Taking a slow breath, she looks up at the other woman, her voice trembling with both hope and certainty.

"I'm ready. I want to open my heart," she says.

The second woman's expression softens, her heart full of affection and joy for this moment. She leans in slightly, offering her support in the most heartfelt way.

"Then let's pray together," she says, her voice full of compassion. "Jesus is waiting for you. All you need to do is ask."

The first woman closes her eyes, feeling a sense of calm descend upon her. This moment feels sacred—like something inside her is shifting, and she is finally letting go of the weight that has burdened her. She joins in, bowing her head slightly, ready to make the most important step of her life.

"Dear Heavenly Father," the second woman prays softly, her voice steady and confident. "We come before You today with open hearts, seeking Your love, Your grace, and Your forgiveness. We thank You for Your Son, Jesus, who died for our sins and made a way for us to be reconciled with You. We ask for Your presence to fill this heart, to guide her in Your truth, and to walk with her every day. We thank You for the new life she is stepping into today. In Jesus' name, Amen."

The room is filled with a holy stillness as the prayer concludes. The first woman feels a surge of emotion rise within her, her heart now lighter than it has ever been. The prayer, the words, the promise—everything feels like it has changed in an instant. A tear slips down her cheek, but it's not from sorrow. It's from the overwhelming joy of finding a path she knows will lead her to peace.

"Thank you. Thank you so much," she says, her voice full of emotion.

The second woman smiles softly, her eyes brimming with love and pride for this decision. This is just the beginning, but she knows it's the most beautiful beginning the first woman could ever have.

"You've made the best decision of your life," she says, her voice full of affection. "Jesus is with you, always. He will guide you, and He will never leave you."

The first woman wipes her eyes, a tearful but contented smile on her face. She feels different. The change is subtle, but it's there. She knows this is just the first step, but she feels confident that she's heading in the right direction. As she glances at the open Bible on the table, she realizes that this decision, this moment, is the beginning of a new chapter—one that is full of hope, grace, and a future that is brighter than she ever imagined.

"I feel… I feel like something inside me has changed," she says, the shift within her undeniable.

The second woman nods, her heart swelling with joy. She's seen it before—the first signs of the Holy Spirit's work in someone's life. This is a moment of transformation, a moment to be cherished.

"That's the Holy Spirit," she says softly. "He's already at work in you. Trust Him, and He will lead you every step of the way."

The first woman nods, the weight of the reassurance grounding her. For the first time, she feels at peace with her decision. She knows this journey won't always be easy, but now she has the strength, the faith, and the support she needs. As she glances at the open Bible, she realizes that this decision, this moment, is the start of something new—something truly beautiful.

Mrs. Thompson beams, her eyes brimming with joy as she watches Sarah wipe a tear from her cheek. The warmth in the room seems to grow, as if the air itself is filled with a divine presence.

"Oh, praise God!" she exclaims with a heartfelt, enthusiastic joy. "This is the best decision you'll ever make, Sarah. I can already see His love shining in you."

Sarah smiles, the tear still lingering on her cheek, but it's no longer one of sadness—it's a tear of relief, of something new blooming within her. She feels lighter, like a weight she didn't even know she was carrying has been lifted. For the first time in a long while, she feels a deep sense of peace, almost like everything in her life has suddenly found its rightful place.

"I… I don't even know how to describe it," Sarah says softly, her voice trembling with emotion. "I just feel different."

Mrs. Thompson's smile widens, her eyes full of tenderness. "That's the Holy Spirit working in you, Sarah. You've made the best decision of your life, and I know He is going to walk with you every step of the way. This is just the beginning of your new life with Him."

Sarah nods slowly, absorbing the words, letting them settle into her heart. A quiet assurance fills her chest as she holds Mrs. Thompson's hands, feeling a connection that goes beyond the physical. It's as though something deep inside her has awakened, something she never even realized she needed.

Mrs. Thompson, still holding Sarah's hands, leans forward a little, her voice becoming more earnest. "You're not alone in this, Sarah. No matter what you face, you have a family here. And most importantly, you have Jesus with you. He'll never leave you."

Sarah's breath catches in her throat, the truth of those words sinking in. She hadn't realized how desperately she needed this kind of assurance until this very moment. The weight of her past struggles seems lighter now, almost insignificant, as she realizes that the journey ahead isn't one she has to face on her own.

"I can't thank you enough," Sarah whispers, her voice thick with emotion. "For being here for me… for guiding me."

Mrs. Thompson shakes her head, her expression soft with understanding. "Sarah, this isn't just me. It's God's work, and I'm so blessed to be a part of it. But I'm here, always. We're a family now, and we'll walk this path together."

The room feels even more peaceful now, the quiet glow of sunlight filtering through the curtains. For the first time, Sarah feels truly embraced—by faith, by Mrs. Thompson, and by the

God she's just invited into her heart. It's an overwhelming feeling, and yet, it's the most comforting thing she's ever known.

As the prayer settles in her heart, Sarah takes a deep breath, a slow but steady exhale. "I'm ready. I'm ready to follow Him."

Mrs. Thompson's eyes shine as she pats Sarah's hands gently. "And you'll never be alone, dear. He's always with you, guiding you. I know He's going to do amazing things through you."

The two of them sit there for a moment, the quiet radiance of the room filling them both with a sense of divine presence. Sarah's heart, once so burdened with confusion and doubt, now feels sure, centered. She knows her life has just taken a turn toward something extraordinary, something she never expected—but always needed.

"Thank you," Sarah says, her voice softer now, full of gratitude. "Thank you for everything."

Mrs. Thompson smiles, squeezing Sarah's hands one last time before letting go. "I'm just happy to be here with you. Remember, if you ever need anything, I'm here. And I'll be praying for you every day."

As Sarah rises, she feels a sense of purpose and belonging that she has never experienced before. Mrs. Thompson stands with her, offering a final embrace that feels like the warmest, most comforting hug. It's the kind of hug that makes her feel like she's truly home—where she belongs.

"I'll keep you in my prayers, always," Mrs. Thompson says gently, her voice full of love.

"Thank you," Sarah says again, her heart full of a deep, abiding peace. "I'm not sure what comes next, but I know now that I'm not walking it alone."

The two share a final smile before Sarah steps toward the door, her spirit lifted, her heart full of new hope. As she steps out into the world, everything seems different—brighter, lighter, filled with possibility. For the first time in a long time, she feels truly at peace, knowing that she has made the most important decision of her life.

Mrs. Thompson nods, her voice softening as she speaks, the weight of her words settling heavily in the room.

"Yes, Marcus. You know, he's not always outwardly expressive about his faith, but he cares deeply for Jasmine. He's been praying for her, too. He believes that one day, she'll come to understand what we have."

Sarah, taken aback by the mention of Marcus's involvement, looks at Mrs. Thompson with curiosity.

"Wow, I didn't know Marcus was so... invested in this," Sarah says, a small smile forming on her lips. "It's kind of surprising, isn't it? He doesn't seem the type to get so involved with faith, but I guess people have their ways of showing it."

Mrs. Thompson's gaze softens as she reflects on the dynamics of her family. "You're right. Marcus doesn't wear his faith on his sleeve, but he's always been a quiet, steady presence. He understands the importance of prayer, even if he doesn't always express it the way others might." She pauses, the sadness returning to her eyes. "As for Jasmine... sometimes, I wonder if we've done enough. If we've shown her enough love, enough grace. But I trust God's timing. He's the one who can change hearts."

Sarah leans forward, her expression filled with empathy. "I get it. It's hard, watching someone you love be so distant from something that brings you peace. But I think, in her own way, Jasmine will come around. You just have to keep being the example, and when the time is right, she'll see the love that's waiting for her."

Mrs. Thompson nods slowly, a bittersweet smile touching her lips. "I hope you're right, Sarah. I hope you're right."

A heavy silence fills the room as the two women sit there, each lost in her thoughts. The weight of the conversation lingers in the air, but there's also a sense of hope, a quiet understanding that, even in the face of uncertainty, faith has the power to transform lives.

Finally, Sarah breaks the silence, her voice soft but firm. "You know, I think Jasmine just needs to experience what we have. She needs to see the peace, the joy, the love that comes from knowing Jesus. Maybe she just hasn't been ready yet. But when she sees it in you, and in Marcus, maybe that will be the turning point."

Mrs. Thompson looks up, her eyes brightening with a flicker of hope. "I hope so. I really do. Sometimes, I just need to remind myself that it's not about pushing or forcing her, it's about letting her come to it in her own time. God knows her heart, even when we don't understand."

Sarah reaches over and places a comforting hand on Mrs. Thompson's. "You've done so much already, Mrs. Thompson. You've shown her love, and that's the most important thing. She'll feel it when she's ready. Just keep praying. Keep being the light."

Mrs. Thompson smiles, her heart warmed by Sarah's words. "Thank you, Sarah. You've given me some peace just now. I'll keep praying. I'll keep believing."

The room feels lighter as the conversation shifts, the shared moment of understanding between them offering both women a sense of comfort. As Sarah takes a deep breath, she feels that sense of peace once again, the same peace that has filled her heart since she made the decision to embrace her faith. She knows, deep down, that this journey is just beginning—for both herself and for Jasmine.

"You know," Sarah says with a thoughtful smile, "maybe one day, Jasmine will come to church with us. I don't know when, but I have a feeling that it will happen. And when it does, she'll know it's because of your prayers, your love, and your faith that she found her way."

Mrs. Thompson's face lights up, her eyes glistening with tears of gratitude. "I pray that day comes soon, Sarah. Thank you for reminding me to have faith, even when it feels hard."

The two women sit together in the quiet warmth of the room, a sense of connection and hope settling over them. As the sunlight continues to filter through the curtains, casting its golden glow on the pages of the Bible, both Sarah and Mrs. Thompson know that the power of prayer, love, and faith will continue to guide them, no matter the challenges they face. And one day, they trust that Jasmine, too, will feel the embrace of that same love.

Mrs. Thompson's expression softens with a touch of sadness as she looks down, reflecting on the past.

"I hoped so too," she admits quietly. "But Jasmine... she's always been so focused on other things. I don't know. Maybe she just doesn't see him the way he sees her. Or maybe she's scared of what it means."

Sarah nods, her face reflecting both sympathy and understanding. "I get it. Sometimes, people don't realize what they have until it's too late. But Marcus... he's never given up, has he?"

Mrs. Thompson smiles softly, though there's a trace of melancholy in her eyes. "No, he hasn't. He's always been persistent, always caring. He truly loves her. But I just wonder... is she ready to see that?"

Sarah leans forward, her voice filled with empathy. "Maybe she will, in time. People change, you know. I think Marcus is just waiting for the right moment. And maybe... maybe Jasmine will see what's been right in front of her all along."

Mrs. Thompson sighs deeply, her hands folded in her lap as she contemplates Sarah's words. "I pray that's true. I really do. She deserves to be loved, to see what Marcus has always offered her."

There's a moment of quiet reflection between them, as they both sit in thought, hoping that one day, Jasmine will come to realize the love that's been patiently waiting for her.

Chapter 18

The dim lighting of the room cast long, stretching shadows across the sleek furniture, making the house feel colder than it actually was. The walls, lined with modern art and expensive decor, seemed almost too pristine, too sterile. A faint hum of silence enveloped the space, broken only by the quiet clicking of footsteps as Trey paced back and forth across the room. His mood was palpable—dark, suffocating—and Jasmine could feel the tension thickening in the air.

Sitting nervously on the couch, her fingers curled around the fabric of her dress, Jasmine felt a knot in her stomach that had been growing for the past few minutes. Her mind raced, unable to focus on anything but the way Trey's movements became sharper, more erratic. The air between them was electric, heavy with an unsaid anger that made her want to shrink further into the cushion.

Without realizing it, she shifted too quickly, knocking over a glass of water on the coffee table. The sound of the glass tumbling, then spilling the liquid, startled her. The water splashed over the edge, pooling onto the surface of the table, a small symbol of her clumsiness.

"Oh, I'm sorry—" she started, her voice already trembling as she reached instinctively for the glass.

But before she could even finish her apology, Trey whirled around. His face was twisted in fury, his jaw clenched tightly, and his eyes—those cold, fiery eyes—locked onto hers with a look that made her stomach churn.

"You can't do anything right, can you?" Trey's voice was a harsh growl, filled with so much anger that it seemed to vibrate through the walls. The words cut through the air like a blade, and Jasmine froze, her pulse spiking. She felt as though the ground beneath her was shifting, her legs no longer able to hold her steady.

Her heart hammered in her chest, and she could feel her breath quickening as she stammered out an explanation.

"It was just a mistake, I didn't mean to—"

Before she could say anything else, before she could try to reason with him, Trey's anger seemed to boil over. His eyes darkened even further, and in one swift movement, he stepped toward her, raising his hand with terrifying speed.

The slap that followed felt like an explosion. A deafening crack rang through the room, loud enough to make her ears buzz. Her head snapped to the side from the force, her cheek instantly burning, the sting searing into her skin. Jasmine gasped, her breath caught in her throat as she instinctively raised a hand to her cheek, her fingers trembling against the heat.

For a moment, the room fell eerily silent. She could hear her heartbeat pounding in her ears, the rush of blood filling her face as her vision blurred from the shock. Her lip trembled as she fought the urge to cry, the pain of the slap mixing with a deeper, more unsettling pain in her chest.

"You're useless," Trey's voice was ice-cold now, almost devoid of emotion. He stood in front of her, his posture stiff and unforgiving. "Can't even handle yourself without messing up. What makes you think you deserve all this?"

His words sliced through her like a blade. The anger in his tone was palpable, and with each sentence, it felt like he was tearing her down piece by piece. She tried to hold back the tears that burned in her eyes, but they came anyway, spilling down her cheeks despite her best efforts to stay composed. Her body felt heavy with the weight of his words, and she couldn't help but flinch as she backed away from him, her movements robotic, as if her body was betraying her.

Her legs were shaky, her knees threatening to buckle beneath her. The door, a few steps away, seemed like the only way out of this nightmare. Without thinking, she stumbled back toward it, her hand still pressed against her cheek, the throbbing ache pulsing with each passing second.

Trey didn't move. He didn't even look at her, his eyes cold, focused on nothing. He just stood there, arms crossed, his body rigid as if he were waiting for her to do something—anything— that would please him. Jasmine reached for the door handle, her breath coming in ragged gasps as she turned the knob, her fingers slipping with the wetness of her own tears.

The air in the room felt suffocating, pressing down on her chest, but all she could think about was getting away—getting out. She opened the door, the cold air of the night outside a sharp contrast to the suffocating heat of the room. Without looking back, she stepped into the hallway, the door swinging shut behind her with a soft click.

Her cheek burned, but it wasn't just the physical pain that overwhelmed her. It was the emotional weight, the deep sense of betrayal and humiliation that settled in her chest. Jasmine's heart ached, a pain that seemed to ripple through every part of her. She had never felt so small, so helpless, in her entire life.

Tears streamed down her face as she walked down the hallway, each step heavier than the last. She didn't know where she was going—only that she needed to escape, to get away from the man who had made her feel less than human. The sting of his words lingered, far more painful than the slap itself.

Jasmine stood frozen in the doorway, her hand still gripping the handle. The sharp sting of the slap was still fresh on her cheek, but it was nothing compared to the emotional turmoil swirling inside her. Her heart was heavy, her chest tight, as her mind ran in circles. Her fingers trembled on the door handle, the weight of the decision pressing down on her. The thought of walking out, leaving the chaos behind, almost felt like a relief.

But then the weight of everything Trey had promised her— the money, the fame, the lifestyle she'd always dreamed of—pulled her back. She had spent so long chasing these things, believing they were the key to her happiness. The thought of losing all that was terrifying. She bit her lip, torn between her self-respect and the overwhelming temptation to stay.

"I can't believe you..." she whispered, her voice thick with emotion. The words felt heavy, like they were stuck in her throat. She felt betrayed, humiliated, yet still tied to him by the promises he'd made.

Without waiting for a response, she grabbed her bag, making a move toward the door as if trying to break free. The very idea of leaving felt freeing, but also suffocating. She was torn.

Trey's voice suddenly sliced through the silence, cruel and unyielding.

"Go ahead, walk out. See how far you get without me."

His words were laced with venom, and they hit her like a slap in the face all over again. She froze at the sound, her body tense with hesitation. Her hand hovered over the door handle, but she couldn't bring herself to leave. The tension in the room was suffocating, and the pull to stay was stronger than the desire to walk away. Her heart was in pieces, torn between her dignity and the life she had become accustomed to.

She hesitated for a moment longer, her thoughts racing. But in the end, she couldn't bring herself to leave him. The reality of walking out on Trey—of leaving everything she thought she needed—was too overwhelming.

Her voice barely rose above a whisper, filled with guilt and uncertainty. "I didn't mean to upset you..." she murmured, her face still flushed from the slap, eyes brimming with unshed tears.

Trey, arms crossed and standing in the middle of the room, didn't soften his gaze. His face was hard, his expression cold and unforgiving, like he was the one in control here. He didn't care about her apology, and that was evident.

"Get back in here," he ordered, his tone sharp and domineering. It was a command, not a request. His words were heavy, loaded with a power that made Jasmine feel small, insignificant.

Jasmine's body responded before her mind could catch up. She stared at the door for one last moment, the air around her thick with tension, her hand still gripping the doorknob. For a brief second, she wondered if she could find the strength to walk away, to break free from the cycle that had her trapped.

But in the end, she turned slowly, as if an invisible force was pulling her back inside. Her shoulders slumped, and her eyes dropped to the floor, defeated. The hope of escaping the suffocating grip of her situation faded with every step she took back into the room.

Trey watched her, his gaze cold and calculating. His cruel smirk returned, curling at the edges of his lips as he saw her comply. There was satisfaction in his eyes now, the power he held over her evident in the way he watched her approach. The smirk on his lips widened slightly, knowing that Jasmine was his again, at least for the moment.

Jasmine walked back into the room, her steps slow and heavy with defeat. Every part of her screamed to leave, to escape, but she couldn't. Not yet.

Trey's smirk deepens, the cruel satisfaction evident in his eyes as he watches Jasmine comply.

"That's more like it," he says, his voice dripping with condescension.

Jasmine lowers her head, her gaze fixated on the floor, a sense of shame washing over her. Her heart aches, the weight of everything crashing down on her—confusion, fear, helplessness. She had hoped for something different, something more, but all she was left with was this.

She walks back to the couch, every step feeling heavier than the last, the pit in her stomach deepening. She sits down, her body tense, her mind spinning with thoughts of escape that never seem possible.

Without warning, Trey steps forward, his hand reaching out to grab her chin roughly. The sudden touch forces her to lift her eyes, her gaze meeting his with reluctance. She can't avoid it now, his commanding presence making her feel small, like a child being scolded.

"You do what I say, when I say it. Got it?" His words come out with an icy, commanding tone, cold and authoritative.

Jasmine's breath catches in her throat, the intensity of his grip on her chin sending a shiver through her. She nods slowly, barely able to find her voice beneath the weight of his dominance.

"Yes..." she whispers, the word heavy with submission.

Trey releases her chin, almost casually, as if the moment meant nothing to him. He turns his attention back to his phone, dismissing her entirely, as though everything that just happened was trivial.

Jasmine is left sitting there, her body numb, her thoughts spiraling. She feels as if she's been shattered into pieces, each one of her emotions buried under layers of fear and self-doubt. The silence between them is deafening, and yet, it's the only sound she can hear.

She's trapped in this toxic cycle—her heart torn between wanting to leave and the suffocating grip of control and fear that keeps her from doing so. The confusion lingers, but it's overshadowed by the hollow emptiness that now resides within her. She wonders how long she can keep pretending that this is okay, that this is what she deserves.

Early in the day, Jasmine steps through the front door into her home, her posture slumped, a heavy weariness in her expression. She drags her feet across the floor, her mind elsewhere. She's wearing a loose shirt, but it doesn't hide the large, jagged scar on her forearm—red, angry, and glaringly obvious against her pale skin. The pain from it still lingers, but it's nothing compared to the emotional turmoil swirling within her.

As soon as Mrs. Thompson, sitting on the couch, sees Jasmine enter, her eyes lock onto the scar. The warmth in her gaze falters as concern quickly replaces it. She stands up, a sudden rush of worry flooding her features.

"Jasmine! What on earth happened to your arm?" Mrs. Thompson's voice is a mix of shock and confusion, her eyes wide as she takes in the sight of the injury.

Jasmine glances down at her arm, her heart skipping a beat as she sees the mark. She quickly looks away, unwilling to meet her mother's gaze. She's practiced at this—pretending that everything's fine, hiding the truth. She shrugs nonchalantly, though the gesture is forced, lacking the confidence it once had.

"It's nothing, Mom," Jasmine mutters, her voice hollow. "Just... an accident."

The words slip out easily, but they feel foreign on her tongue. She knows it's a lie, but it's the only thing she can offer, the only thing that keeps the question from digging any deeper. Jasmine avoids eye contact, knowing that if she looked at her mother, she'd see the truth—the hurt, the exhaustion, the conflict inside her that she's struggling to hide.

Mrs. Thompson's eyes narrow with concern, but she doesn't press further. She watches her daughter carefully, sensing the distance, but also knowing that Jasmine is hiding something she's not ready to share. The silence stretches, heavy and thick, between them. The scar on Jasmine's arm is just one of many things she's trying to keep hidden, but the emotional scars are harder to mask.

Mrs. Thompson stands up, her movements swift with concern. She steps closer to Jasmine, her eyes never leaving the scar, which seems to pulse with an almost sinister presence. The concern on her face deepens as she reaches out, trying to get a closer look at the injury.

"That's not nothing," Mrs. Thompson insists, her voice trembling slightly with worry. "That looks serious! How did this happen?"

Jasmine flinches slightly at her mother's touch, her body instinctively recoiling. She tugs her sleeve down over the scar, desperately trying to hide it, as though it might erase the conversation, the attention, the scrutiny. Her face hardens, a defensive mask slipping into place. She turns her body away, not willing to face the full force of her mother's concern.

"I said it's nothing! Just leave it, okay?" Jasmine snaps, her voice cold and distant, an edge of frustration creeping into her tone. She clenches her jaw, willing her mother to drop it, to let her carry this burden alone.

But Mrs. Thompson isn't so easily deterred. Her eyes narrow, not out of anger, but out of worry, a deep motherly instinct to protect her daughter. She senses there's more to this than Jasmine is willing to admit. The evasiveness, the defensiveness—it all tells her that something is wrong, something beyond just a simple accident.

Jasmine feels her mother's eyes on her back, the silent question hanging in the air. She can feel the weight of it pressing down on her, but she keeps her gaze fixed on the floor, wishing she could make herself disappear.

Mrs. Thompson watches with a growing sense of helplessness as Jasmine stands there, her eyes darting around the room, avoiding her gaze. She can see the tension in her daughter's posture, the tightness in her jaw, the subtle tremble in her hands that Jasmine tries so hard to hide. The scar, the obvious sign of something much more than a simple accident, is a silent cry for help, one that Mrs. Thompson can't ignore.

"Jasmine..." she begins softly, her voice trembling with motherly concern. "You know you can talk to me, right? If something—if someone—"

Before she can finish her sentence, Jasmine whirls around sharply, cutting her off with a raw, almost bitter tone.

"I said it's fine! Stop making a big deal out of everything!" Jasmine's voice rings out with an edge that seems to slice through the room. Her words, biting and defensive, hang in the air. She stands there, breathing heavily, her chest rising and falling as though her outburst has taken something out of her.

Mrs. Thompson's heart sinks at the harshness of Jasmine's words. She hadn't expected the anger, the defensiveness—certainly not in response to her concern. Her face falls, the hurt visible in the way her shoulders slump. She wanted so much to ease Jasmine's pain, to help her, but this barrier, this wall her daughter has built, makes it feel impossible.

"I... I didn't mean to upset you," Mrs. Thompson says quietly, her voice softening, the words carrying more weight than they might seem. She reaches a tentative hand towards Jasmine, but it hovers in the air, unsure, uncertain of how much more to press.

Jasmine, visibly frustrated, clenches her fists at her sides, her nails digging into her palms as if it might keep her from breaking down. She shakes her head, a faint sigh escaping her lips, but it's not relief—it's the sound of a soul at war.

"I just need some space, Mom," Jasmine mutters, her voice quieter now but still laced with frustration. Without waiting for a response, she turns on her heel, moving swiftly toward her room. Her steps are purposeful, almost mechanical, as though she's trying to outrun the conversation, the worry, the fear that has settled over her.

Mrs. Thompson stands frozen in place, her hand still suspended in the air as if reaching for something she can't quite grasp. The silence that follows is thick and heavy, the sound of her daughter's retreating footsteps echoing in her ears.

"I'm just worried about you, Jasmine..." she calls after her, her voice barely above a whisper, thick with unspoken emotion. Her words hang in the air, a soft plea for her daughter to hear her, to understand that the concern runs deeper than just the scar or the argument. It's the years of love, of sacrifice, of watching Jasmine grow into the young woman she is, and fearing that something is slipping through her fingers, something she can't quite reach.

Jasmine doesn't respond. She doesn't even slow down. The sound of the door to her room closing gently is the only answer Mrs. Thompson receives, and it cuts through the room like a quiet, final blow.

Mrs. Thompson stands there for a long moment, her gaze fixed on the hallway where her daughter just disappeared. Her heart aches, the worry in her chest swelling as she contemplates what's really going on inside Jasmine's heart and mind. What is her daughter hiding? What pain is she carrying alone?

Mrs. Thompson's sigh is heavy, filled with the weight of unanswered questions. She knows she has to be patient, but it's becoming harder with each passing day. Still, she holds onto hope—hope that one day, Jasmine will open up, that she will come to her for help, and that together, they can face whatever is haunting her. Until then, all Mrs. Thompson can do is wait and pray.

Chapter 19

Mrs. Thompson remains on her knees, the quiet hum of the night surrounding her like a blanket. Her hands are clasped tightly together, knuckles white with the intensity of her grip. Her eyes are closed, her face a portrait of deep concentration and sorrow. The weight of her worry about Jasmine seems to fill the room, but she presses on, pouring her heart into the prayer, a steady whisper that trembles with emotion.

"Lord, I lift Jasmine up to You," she begins, her voice barely audible, but filled with an undeniable sincerity. "I don't know what's happening in her life right now, but You do." Her words, raw and filled with love, spill out with an urgency that comes from a mother's heart, desperate for answers. Her brow furrows as she leans into her prayer, feeling a deep ache within her chest that only God can understand. "I ask for Your protection over her, God. Soften her heart, Lord, and bring her back to You. I know You have plans for her, and I trust You, Father."

As she speaks, the words are not just a request; they are a plea, a cry for her daughter's well-being, for her salvation. The tears that have been gathering in her eyes now begin to fall freely, streaking down her cheeks as they mix with her fervent prayers. Her hands tremble slightly, the weight of her worries adding to the burden that she's carried in silence for so long.

"Please, save her, guide her, and let her see the truth before it's too late," she continues, her voice breaking with emotion. "Please, Lord, show her the way back to You. I can't do this on my own. I need You."

Her words, drenched in both sorrow and hope, are a cry of a mother who feels helpless yet refuses to let go of her faith. The words are barely a whisper now, but they are filled with a deep, quiet conviction that only a mother could possess. Her tears fall freely, but she doesn't stop praying, her heart steadfast in its belief, even though the weight of the world seems to rest on her shoulders.

"In Jesus' name, I believe. Amen."

As she finishes, the last word hanging in the air, she takes a shuddering breath and wipes the tears from her cheeks. She looks down at her hands, resting gently on the Bible in front of her. The silence in the room is almost suffocating, but it's also a peace—a quiet acceptance that she has done what she can, and now, she must trust God to handle the rest.

Mrs. Thompson slowly rises to her feet, her legs stiff from kneeling for so long. She walks to the edge of the bed, her heart still heavy, but also grounded in the strength of her faith. She sits down, her hands resting on her lap as she gazes down at the open Bible. The words she just prayed echo in her mind, the weight of the prayer still pressing against her heart.

For a moment, she simply sits there in the stillness, allowing herself to reflect. Her mind drifts to thoughts of Jasmine—her daughter, so lost, so far away from the path she once walked. The thought brings more tears, but Mrs. Thompson refuses to let despair take hold. She knows that God's timing is beyond understanding, and she holds on to that truth with all the strength she has left.

She lets out a long sigh, her chest tightening with the unspoken fears she hasn't shared with anyone. There's so much she doesn't know about what Jasmine is going through, so much pain that is buried deep inside her daughter. But Mrs. Thompson holds onto hope, to faith, knowing that her prayers are heard, and she believes, with every fiber of her being, that Jasmine will find her way back to God's light.

And so, with a heart that is heavy but resolute, Mrs. Thompson silently rises from the bed and prepares for whatever the next day will bring. She knows her journey as a mother, and as a woman of faith, is far from over.

Mrs. Thompson remains on her knees, the quiet hum of the night surrounding her like a blanket. Her hands are clasped tightly together, knuckles white with the intensity of her grip. Her eyes are closed, her face a portrait of deep concentration and sorrow. The weight of her worry about Jasmine seems to fill the room, but she presses on, pouring her heart into the prayer, a steady whisper that trembles with emotion.

"Lord, I lift Jasmine up to You," she begins, her voice barely audible, but filled with an undeniable sincerity. "I don't know what's happening in her life right now, but You do." Her words, raw and filled with love, spill out with an urgency that comes from a mother's heart, desperate for answers. Her brow furrows as she leans into her prayer, feeling a deep ache within her chest that only God can understand. "I ask for Your protection over her, God. Soften her heart, Lord, and bring her back to You. I know You have plans for her, and I trust You, Father."

As she speaks, the words are not just a request; they are a plea, a cry for her daughter's well-being, for her salvation. The tears that have been gathering in her eyes now begin to fall freely, streaking down her cheeks as they mix with her fervent prayers. Her hands tremble slightly, the weight of her worries adding to the burden that she's carried in silence for so long.

"Please, save her, guide her, and let her see the truth before it's too late," she continues, her voice breaking with emotion. "Please, Lord, show her the way back to You. I can't do this on my own. I need You."

Her words, drenched in both sorrow and hope, are a cry of a mother who feels helpless yet refuses to let go of her faith. The words are barely a whisper now, but they are filled with a deep, quiet conviction that only a mother could possess. Her tears fall freely, but she doesn't stop praying, her heart steadfast in its belief, even though the weight of the world seems to rest on her shoulders.

"In Jesus' name, I believe. Amen."

As she finishes, the last word hanging in the air, she takes a shuddering breath and wipes the tears from her cheeks. She looks down at her hands, resting gently on the Bible in front of her. The silence in the room is almost suffocating, but it's also a peace—a quiet acceptance that she has done what she can, and now, she must trust God to handle the rest.

Mrs. Thompson slowly rises to her feet, her legs stiff from kneeling for so long. She walks to the edge of the bed, her heart still heavy, but also grounded in the strength of her faith. She sits down, her hands resting on her lap as she gazes down at the open Bible. The words she just prayed echo in her mind, the weight of the prayer still pressing against her heart.

For a moment, she simply sits there in the stillness, allowing herself to reflect. Her mind drifts to thoughts of Jasmine—her daughter, so lost, so far away from the path she once walked. The thought brings more tears, but Mrs. Thompson refuses to let despair take hold. She knows that God's timing is beyond understanding, and she holds on to that truth with all the strength she has left.

She lets out a long sigh, her chest tightening with the unspoken fears she hasn't shared with anyone. There's so much she doesn't know about what Jasmine is going through, so much pain that is buried deep inside her daughter. But Mrs. Thompson holds onto hope, to faith, knowing that her prayers are heard, and she believes, with every fiber of her being, that Jasmine will find her way back to God's light.

And so, with a heart that is heavy but resolute, Mrs. Thompson silently rises from the bed and prepares for whatever the next day will bring. She knows her journey as a mother, and as a woman of faith, is far from over.

Marcus sits in the quiet solitude of his modest apartment, the soft glow of the overhead light casting a peaceful, almost reverent atmosphere. The room is sparsely decorated, with only the bare essentials—a couch, a small coffee table, and a few personal items scattered about, creating a sense of simplicity and reflection. The air is still, as if the space itself holds its breath, waiting for the weight of his thoughts to settle.

He's hunched over, elbows resting on his knees, his posture slumped yet steady, as though the weight of his emotions is too much for him to bear but he refuses to let it overwhelm him completely. His hands are clasped tightly in front of him, fingers interlaced, and his gaze is fixed downward, his eyes closed as he silently prays. The quiet of the apartment amplifies the depth of his prayer, every breath he takes measured, slow, deliberate, as if each one is an offering to God.

Beside him, on the couch, rests his Bible, open to a passage that he's been reading for some time, though it's clear that his attention isn't entirely on the words before him. The Bible has become his anchor, a constant in the midst of his uncertainty, the foundation on which he leans when everything else feels uncertain.

His lips move slightly as he prays, the words barely audible, yet the intensity of his prayer fills the room with a sense of solemnity. He prays not just for himself, but for others—his family, his friends, and especially for the one who weighs most heavily on his heart: Jasmine. His heart aches for her, his prayers filled with hope and desperation. He asks God for wisdom, for strength, for guidance, not only for himself but for Jasmine, praying that she finds her way out of the darkness that seems to surround her.

Tears threaten to fall, but Marcus holds them back, his chest tight as he wrestles with his emotions. He knows he can't change everything, but he believes that God can. He's been praying for Jasmine for so long, and he feels as though every prayer is a step toward something greater, something more significant than he could ever achieve on his own. The silence of the room presses in on him, but in this silence, he finds a connection, a deep intimacy with God.

The minutes tick by, but Marcus remains unmoving, his heart laid bare in this vulnerable moment of faith. When he finally opens his eyes, they are filled with a quiet resolve, a strength that seems to come from the very core of his being. He slowly reaches for the Bible beside him, gently closing it as he offers one last, quiet prayer.

"Lord, I trust You," he whispers, his voice steady despite the emotions swirling inside him. "Please, guide her back. Please, let her see the truth."

With that, Marcus stands up slowly, his movements deliberate as he takes a deep breath and looks out the window, his heart still heavy but now anchored in a deeper peace. He knows that his journey is far from over, but he is willing to wait, to pray, and to trust in God's plan for Jasmine, even if it takes time.

Marcus sits in the stillness of his apartment, the weight of his thoughts heavy on his chest. The air feels thick with the urgency of his prayer, as though every word he speaks is an offering to the God he trusts with his deepest emotions. He closes his eyes again, his hands clasped tightly in front of him, as if holding on to the very words that could change everything.

MARCUS

(whispering, his voice filled with longing)

"Lord, it's been so long since Jasmine and I talked, but I know You're still watching over her. I pray for her, God... I pray that whatever she's going through, You'd protect her. Open her eyes, Lord. Help her see what's right, and bring her back from wherever she is right now. I'm trusting You to do a miracle in her life."

His voice cracks slightly as he speaks, the vulnerability in his words palpable. His brow furrows as the weight of the past and the uncertainty of the future press upon him. A deep, aching silence follows, his thoughts consumed by Jasmine, the girl he's loved for so long, but who seems so distant now. His heart tightens as he remembers the way she used to be—the girl full of life, full of laughter, before everything began to change. The hope that she might find her way back fills him with both anticipation and fear.

MARCUS (CONT'D)

(softly, his voice thick with emotion)

"I still care for her, Lord. You know that. Please, let her feel Your love. And if there's anything I can do, show me, God. I want to help her."

(he pauses, his voice becoming quieter, almost a whisper)

"In Jesus' name, amen."

As the final words leave his lips, Marcus takes a long, slow breath, the heaviness in his chest not quite lifted, but softened by the act of surrender. He opens his eyes, blinking away the tears that threaten to form, and looks down at the Bible resting in front of him. His fingers gently trace the edges of the pages, his touch light, as though the very book he's holding contains the answers he's searching for.

Marcus takes a moment to reflect on the prayer he just offered, letting the words settle in his heart. There is no immediate answer, no sign of what comes next—but somehow, the peace of his prayer begins to fill the space around him. He sighs deeply, allowing the stillness to wash over him, his mind and heart finding some small measure of comfort in the belief that, no matter what happens, God is in control.

With a deep exhale, he finally stands, feeling a quiet strength rise within him. He looks out the window, the faint glow of the streetlights outside casting soft shadows into his room. Though the uncertainty remains, Marcus feels a renewed sense of purpose. He doesn't know when or how, but he believes that one day, he will be able to help Jasmine find her way back to herself.

Until then, all he can do is trust and wait, praying with every ounce of his being that she will feel the love he holds for her—and the love God has for her—even from a distance.

Sarah sits in the church pew, her hands gently raised, palms facing upward as the congregation sings a hymn. The melody fills the air, and her face reflects complete peace. Her eyes are closed, and her lips move in silent worship, fully immersed in the presence of God. The atmosphere around her feels sacred, as though time has paused to embrace the moment of devotion. The weight of her faith rests on her shoulders, yet she seems unburdened, her spirit soaring. At home, she sits at her kitchen table, the warm glow of the afternoon sun casting light on the pages of her Bible. Her highlighter moves over the words with purpose, carefully marking verses that resonate deeply within her. Her focus is unwavering, her eyes scanning each passage with intensity. As she reads, she drinks in the Word of God, savoring every revelation, allowing it to nourish her soul. The table is quiet, save for the soft rustling of pages and the occasional scribble of her highlighter, a physical representation of her growing understanding and devotion.

Back at church, after the service, Sarah is seen talking with a small group of believers in the fellowship hall. Her laughter is warm, and her eyes sparkle with genuine joy as she engages in deep conversations about faith. The group gathers around her, drawn to her energy and the wisdom she has gained through her personal journey. There is an air of camaraderie and mutual respect as Sarah listens with a humble heart, sharing her insights and experiences, encouraging others with her words and her presence. In her bedroom, Sarah kneels by her bed, hands clasped in prayer. Her lips move softly, her words inaudible to anyone around, but her heart speaks loudly to God. Her Bible lies open beside her, the pages marked and well-worn, a symbol of the time she has spent in the Word. The room is dimly lit, a peaceful silence enveloping her as she pours out her heart to the Lord. There is a sense of quiet surrender in her posture, a deep connection between her and God, as she seeks His guidance and strength.

Once again in church, Sarah is leading a prayer with her small group. Her voice is strong and confident, a steady reflection of the faith that has blossomed within her. The group listens intently, hanging on her every word as she speaks with passion and conviction. Her faith is radiant, not only in her words but in the way she carries herself, with a quiet authority and grace. It is clear to everyone around her that Sarah's journey has been one of deep transformation, her trust in God shining through in every prayer, every conversation, every action.

She stands front and center, dressed in a flashy, form-fitting outfit that gleams under the bright lights, her makeup flawless and meticulously done. She exudes an air of confidence, but there's a hint of arrogance in her posture. Her attitude is as loud as her ensemble, and she seems completely unaware of the chaos unfolding around her. The crew members, visibly frustrated, scurry about the set, adjusting lights, moving cameras, and fine-tuning props, all while exchanging looks of exhaustion and exasperation. The air is thick with tension as the crew members try to work under the pressure of her demanding behavior.

Chapter 20

A makeup artist, trying to keep up with her ever-evolving look, approaches with a brush to touch up her face. She doesn't even spare her a glance before swatting her hand away dismissively.

"I said I don't need more powder! Are you deaf?" she snaps.

The makeup artist, caught off guard by the harsh tone, retreats without a word, shaking her head in frustration. She rolls her eyes dramatically and tosses her hair back, her fingers running through the locks as she stares into the nearby mirror, admiring herself. Her reflection seems to validate her sense of superiority, feeding her ego.

Meanwhile, the director, growing increasingly agitated by the delays, claps his hands sharply to grab the crew's attention. His voice cuts through the noise of the bustling set.

"Alright, everyone! Let's focus, we're losing time!" he commands.

She barely acknowledges the director, too absorbed in her own image to be bothered by his command. The crew, on edge, exchange glances before continuing their work, trying their best to keep the shoot on track despite the diva-like behavior they have to tolerate.

As the camera starts rolling, she struts confidently through the set, her movements exaggerated and deliberate, posing every few steps and tossing suggestive glances at the camera. Her arrogance is palpable, and it radiates off her in waves. The crew watches from behind the camera, exchanging weary glances, clearly fed up with the act they've been forced to tolerate.

One crew member, Lucy, can no longer keep her frustration in check. She mutters under her breath, loud enough for those nearby to hear.

"She really thinks she's something, doesn't she?"

Another crew member, Chris, visibly irritated and unable to hold back any longer, shoots a glance at Lucy and speaks louder than necessary, his words laced with bitterness.

"She's not even the only one Trey's screwing," he snaps. "There's a line of girls—she's just lucky she's the main one."

Jasmine, in mid-pose, hears the comment. Her smile falters, her body stiffening. She freezes, the air suddenly growing tense around her. Her eyes narrow, seething with anger, as she pivots toward the crew. The confidence in her stance is gone, replaced by pure fury.

"What did you just say?" she demands, her voice icy, cutting through the silence like a blade. The crew falls silent, caught off guard by the sudden shift in her demeanor.

The crew falls into a tense silence, exchanging awkward glances, unsure of how to respond to the confrontation. Chris, however, shrugs nonchalantly, unfazed by Jasmine's outburst.

"You heard me," he says, his tone casual, almost dismissive. "You're not the only one Trey's got his eyes on. He's just keeping you around for now."

Jasmine's face flushes with a mix of fury and hurt. The sting of his words cuts deeper than she's willing to admit, her emotions swirling with a rage she can barely contain. Her hands ball into fists at her sides, and her body trembles with anger. Without a second glance at the crew, she snaps, her voice sharp and bitter.

"I am done with you lot!"

Her words hang in the air as she storms off the set, her heels clicking angrily against the floor. The crew watches her retreat, stunned into silence, the tension still thick in the air long after she's gone.

Jasmine storms down the hallway, her heels clicking against the floor with a sharp, furious rhythm. Her hand grips the door handle, and in one swift motion, she bursts it open, the force of it slamming against the wall.

From her point of view, the room is a scene she never expected to witness, and it hits her like a punch to the gut.

Trey is on the couch, casually relaxed, with a woman perched on his lap. Her arms are draped around his neck, and she's laughing softly, her fingers idly stroking his hair. The sight is too much for Jasmine to process, and her heart drops into her stomach.

The room falls into a heavy, uncomfortable silence. Trey and the woman both look up at the sound of the door, their expressions shifting from surprise to a quick flash of discomfort. The woman scrambles off Trey's lap, her movements flustered as she hurriedly smooths down her dress, her face flushed. Trey remains seated for a beat, an annoyed sigh escaping his lips.

Jasmine stands frozen in the doorway, her heart racing with disbelief and hurt. Trey finally rises from the couch, his irritation evident, but he quickly masks it with a forced calmness, his posture defensive.

"Jazz..." he starts, holding up his hands in an attempt to placate her, "It's not what it looks like."

Jasmine's breath hitches as her voice cracks with the weight of her emotions, the sting of betrayal cutting through her. She can barely hold herself together, her words trembling as she confronts him.

"Not what it looks like?" she repeats, her voice filled with disbelief and a raw, aching hurt. "I can't believe you..."

Jasmine's face flushes bright red, her anger mixing with the deep ache in her chest. The pain of betrayal is so overwhelming, it feels like it's suffocating her. Her breath comes in rapid bursts, her chest rising and falling as she struggles to control the storm of emotions swirling inside her. Her hands tremble slightly at her sides, her fists clenching and unclenching as if the physical action could somehow relieve the tension in her heart. She blinks rapidly, but it's no use—the tears begin to well up in her eyes, threatening to spill over. She can feel the weight of them, a mixture of heartbreak, disbelief, and the fury of being lied to and humiliated all at once. Her stomach twists painfully, the knot of frustration and hurt tightening with every passing second.

Trey steps forward, his movements deliberate, trying to close the space between them, his expression now shifting from defensive to something colder—something manipulative. His voice is calm, almost patronizing as he speaks, attempting to assert control over the situation once again.

"Look, this—this is business," Trey begins, the words slipping off his tongue like a rehearsed lie, his eyes locking onto hers with a forced sincerity. "She means nothing."

The words don't even register at first. Jasmine's brain struggles to make sense of the absurdity of what he's saying. But then, her disbelief overpowers everything. She lets out a bitter laugh, sharp and cutting, the sound of it like a slap to the face. Her laugh is filled with incredulity, the sarcasm and hurt obvious in every strained syllable.

"Business?" Jasmine repeats, her voice thick with disbelief. She shakes her head as if trying to clear it, her eyes narrowing as she takes in the scene—Trey sitting there on the couch with the woman still lingering, her face flushed and eyes downcast, making herself as small as possible. Jasmine can barely hold her composure as she stares at Trey. "You're sitting there with her on your lap, and it's just business?"

The words hang in the air like a heavy weight, each syllable sharper than the last. The woman by the door shifts uncomfortably, her presence now a silent testament to the betrayal, but Jasmine can't even bring herself to care about her. Her focus is solely on Trey—on the man she trusted, the man who had promised her the world, only to tear it apart with one brief, ridiculous explanation.

Trey runs a hand through his hair, a motion that feels tired and rehearsed, like he's trying to keep his calm, but his irritation is starting to show. His patience with her is thinning, and Jasmine can see it in the way his jaw tightens, in the way his shoulders stiffen. But it's not enough to make her back down. It only fuels the fire inside her.

"You're blowing this way out of proportion, Jazz," Trey mutters, his voice clipped, rising in agitation. "You need to calm down."

The words hit her like a slap, the dismissiveness in them cutting deeper than any of the hurtful things he's said so far. Jasmine's entire body stiffens with fury. She can feel her heart pounding in her chest, a wild thud that echoes in her ears. She takes a step forward, closing the distance between them, her face contorted with anger.

"Calm down?" Her voice rises, louder now, every word saturated with the raw pain of betrayal. "You want me to calm down after what I just saw? You think I'm stupid?"

She can't help it—her voice cracks as the rage and the hurt overwhelm her. Her hands fly to her sides, clenched so tightly that her knuckles turn white. The tears threaten again, but she forces them back. Her eyes blaze with a fiery intensity as she glares at Trey, her face a mixture of disbelief and outrage. The man standing in front of her is not the person she thought she knew— he's a stranger, a liar, someone she's never been able to trust, no matter how much she wanted to.

Her voice breaks again, the anger almost choking her as she continues, every word heavy with the weight of betrayal. "You think I'm stupid enough to believe your lies? To let you walk all over me like I'm some idiot?"

Jasmine shakes her head, the movement almost violent, as if she's trying to shake the absurdity of the situation from her mind. She can't process it. She can't understand how everything they had—everything he promised her—could be so easily shattered by his lies. His false assurances, his manipulations. She refuses to let him feed her any more of that nonsense.

"I'm done," she mutters under her breath, but loud enough for him to hear. Her eyes glint with finality as she stands tall, despite the way her heart feels like it's been torn out of her chest. She takes a deep breath, her body trembling with anger and hurt as she takes another step back.

"I'm done with you, Trey." The words are more final than any action she could take. They sting her lips as she says them, but they feel like a release at the same time. She won't stand for this. She won't allow him to treat her like this anymore. His lies, his arrogance, they have no place in her life.

Trey opens his mouth to respond, but Jasmine doesn't give him the chance. She turns, her heels clicking angrily against the floor as she storms out of the room, her emotions a whirlwind inside her. Each step feels like a weight lifting off her shoulders, but the pain in her chest remains, an ache that won't be easily healed. She doesn't know what's next, but she knows one thing for sure—she will never let him do this to her again.

Jasmine's voice cracks as she speaks, barely above a whisper, but the tremble in her words betrays the depth of the pain she's feeling. "I thought you were different..." Her chest tightens with the realization that everything she believed in, everything she thought they had, was just a lie—a façade. Her heart aches with a rawness she can't even put into words.

Before Trey has a chance to say anything, Jasmine whips around and storms out of the room, her body shaking with fury and betrayal. The sound of her heels slamming against the floor is like a drumbeat echoing her anger, her resolve. She doesn't look back—not once. She won't allow herself to linger in that place any longer.

Behind her, Trey remains unmoved, the look on his face almost indifferent. He doesn't understand the weight of her words, the finality in her actions. He watches her leave, his expression one of resignation as if he doesn't really care. As if nothing matters except the moment he's in now. Jasmine doesn't wait for him, doesn't care to hear any more of his empty excuses. She is done.

Jasmine steps out into the street, the cool air hitting her face, but it does nothing to soothe the storm raging inside her. Her mind races, thoughts colliding in a whirlwind of anger, disbelief, and sadness. Her footsteps quicken, matching the chaos in her heart. Every step feels like it's carrying her further away from the man she thought she loved—and every step feels heavier than the last.

Her heart aches, and her mind is clouded with questions she doesn't know how to answer. How could he do this to her? How could he betray her trust so completely? Her body trembles with the emotional weight of it all, but she won't let herself break down—not yet. Not here.

Her eyes sting with unshed tears, the heaviness of them threatening to spill over, but she holds them back. She's not going to cry. Not for him. Not after everything. Jasmine clenches her fists, nails biting into her palms as she fights to regain some control over her emotions. She won't be weak. She won't let him see that he's broken her.

With each step, the world around her feels distant—hazy, as if she's walking through a dream, one she's desperate to wake up from. But the cold reality settles in, and she realizes she's alone. Alone with her hurt, alone with the silence of the streets that seem to mock her as she walks. The emptiness inside her is overwhelming, but the anger—her anger—is what propels her forward. She's angry at him, at herself, at the whole situation.

Jasmine's stride falters for a moment, her vision blurring as she fights against the emotions threatening to surface, but she steels herself again. She wipes away the tear that has escaped, determined not to let anyone see her fall apart. Not when she still has some pride left to hold onto.

She keeps walking, one step after another, through the streets that feel colder and lonelier than ever before.

Mrs. Thompson sits on the well-worn couch, the Bible resting open on her lap, its pages soft from years of prayer and study. The room is bathed in the gentle amber glow of a single lamp, a modest sanctuary from the chaos that seems to have engulfed her family. Her tired eyes drift to the closed door of Jasmine's bedroom. The door, a physical barrier between mother and daughter, feels heavier tonight—symbolizing the emotional distance that has grown between them. Her heart aches with worry, a kind of maternal pain that words can't quite capture.

With a deep sigh, she shifts her position, sliding from the couch to kneel on the floor. Her knees press into the faded rug as she clasps her hands tightly together, resting her forehead against them. The weight of her love for Jasmine mingles with the burden of her helplessness, making her voice tremble as she begins to pray.

"Lord," she whispers, her voice thick with emotion, "I come before You once again, lifting Jasmine up to You. Father, You see her pain. You see her confusion. You know the struggles she's carrying in her heart, even if she doesn't want to share them with me."

Her words falter for a moment as a lump rises in her throat, but she presses on, her emotions spilling over. Tears begin to roll down her cheeks, each one a testament to the countless sleepless nights she's spent worrying about her daughter.

"Father, I'm begging You," she continues, her tone more urgent now, "step into her life. Touch her heart in a way that only You can. Break through the walls she's put up—the ones that are keeping her from seeing Your truth, Your love. Lord, I know You have a plan for her, even when I can't see it, even when it feels like she's slipping further and further away."

She pauses, drawing in a shaky breath. The room feels still, almost sacred, as if her words are filling the air with a quiet reverence. Her fingers clutch the edge of the couch as though holding on to the only anchor she has in this storm.

"God, I know I'm just her mother," she says softly, her voice cracking, "but You're her Creator. You know every thought in her head, every hurt in her heart. You know the things she's chasing after and the emptiness they leave behind. Show her, Lord. Open her eyes to see that nothing out there can ever satisfy her the way You can."

Her hands tighten into fists, her knuckles whitening as the desperation in her voice grows. "And Lord, please give me wisdom. Help me to know how to reach her, how to speak to her without pushing her further away. Help me to show her Your love through my actions, even when it's hard, even when it feels like she doesn't want me around."

Mrs. Thompson lifts her head slightly, her tear-streaked face illuminated by the soft glow of the lamp. She gazes at the ceiling as if searching for a glimpse of God's presence, her eyes full of faith mingled with sorrow.

"I trust You, Lord," she whispers, her tone quieter now, tinged with a fragile hope. "I know You haven't forgotten her. I know You're still working, even when I can't see it. Please, God, bring her back to You. Bring her back to us."

Her voice trails off into silence, but her lips continue to move as she prays silently, pouring out every ounce of her love and concern to the One she believes can make a difference. She stays there for a long moment, her head bowed, the faint sound of her breathing the only noise in the room.

Finally, with a deep, shuddering breath, Mrs. Thompson wipes her face with trembling hands. Her heart still feels heavy, but there's a flicker of peace in her spirit—a quiet assurance that God has heard her prayer. As she rises to her feet, she glances at Jasmine's door one more time, her expression a mixture of hope and determination.

Picking up her Bible, she presses it against her chest and whispers, "Thank You, Lord, for hearing me. I trust You with my daughter."

Chapter 21:

Marcus sits at his desk, the light from his laptop casting a faint glow in the otherwise dim room. The clutter of books, papers, and notes reflects the chaos of his mind, though he barely notices it. His headphones block out the world as his fingers dance across the keyboard, the soft clicks filling the air. Suddenly, his hands freeze, hovering over the keys as an unshakable unease settles in his chest.

His brows furrow as he pulls off the headphones, letting them hang around his neck. He leans back in his chair, rubbing his temples. The feeling is inexplicable but heavy, like a storm brewing in the distance.

"Why do I feel this...?" Marcus mutters under his breath, his voice tinged with confusion. He pushes his chair back and rises, pacing the small confines of the room. Each step seems to match the rhythm of his racing thoughts. He rubs the back of his neck, trying to shake off the unease, but it clings to him like a shadow.

His gaze lands on a picture frame perched on the corner of his desk. The photograph inside is slightly faded but still clear enough to stir something deep within him. It's Jasmine, smiling brightly in a moment captured years ago. She looks carefree, happy—so different from the distant memory of her he's been carrying lately.

Marcus picks up the frame, his thumb brushing over the glass as his expression softens. Concern etches itself into his features as he stares at the picture, his heart tightening.

"Why do I feel a leading to pray for Jasmine?" he asks aloud, his voice barely above a whisper. The question hangs in the air, unanswered but persistent. He exhales deeply, the weight of the moment pressing down on him.

He sets the frame back on the desk and moves to the side of his bed. The cluttered room seems to fade away as he kneels, clasping his hands together. His breathing steadies, and for a moment, he closes his eyes, focusing on the words forming in his heart.

"Lord," Marcus begins, his voice trembling slightly, "I don't know why, but I feel like You're telling me to pray for Jasmine right now. Wherever she is, whatever she's going through... please, be with her."

The words feel both heavy and urgent as they leave his lips. He pauses, his emotions building. He grips his hands tighter, leaning forward as if the posture could somehow carry his prayer further.

"Protect her, Lord," he continues, his voice gaining strength. "Keep her safe from harm. Help her to see the truth, to know her worth, to walk away from anything or anyone that's hurting her."

Memories of Jasmine flood his mind—her laughter, her stubbornness, her moments of vulnerability. He presses his lips together, his chest tightening. He feels a deep, almost painful longing for her to find peace, to find her way back to the light he knows she's drifted from.

"I believe You have something better for her," Marcus says, his tone earnest, almost pleading. "Help her to see that, to feel Your love and guidance. She doesn't need to be caught up in whatever's pulling her away from You. Show her that there's more—so much more."

A lump forms in his throat, but he swallows it down, refusing to let the emotion derail his focus. His hands, still clasped, tremble slightly as he presses them against his forehead.

"Show her the way back to You, God," he says softly, his voice breaking. "Don't let her fall too far. I know You can reach her heart, no matter where she is or what she's going through. You've done it before. Please, do it again."

His voice fades into a whisper as he finishes, the room falling silent save for the faint hum of his laptop and the distant sounds of the night outside. He stays there, kneeling by the bed, his heart heavy but hopeful. The act of praying feels like the only thing he can do—like the only thread of connection he still has to Jasmine.

"Amen," Marcus finally says, the word barely audible as it escapes his lips. He sits back on his heels, his hands lowering to rest on his thighs. His eyes remain closed for a moment longer, his breathing steadying as the intensity of the prayer subsides.

When he opens his eyes, they land once again on the photograph of Jasmine. He picks it up, his fingers tracing the edges of the frame. The weight in his chest hasn't entirely lifted, but there's a flicker of peace—a sense that he's done what he could, that his prayer has been heard.

"Wherever you are, Jazz," he murmurs to the picture, his voice filled with quiet determination, "I'm trusting God to bring you back."

Marcus places the frame gently back on the desk and stands, his mind still swirling with thoughts of Jasmine. He takes a deep breath and exhales slowly, feeling both the burden of his concern and the comfort of his faith. The night stretches on, but he feels a subtle shift within himself—a reassurance that he's not carrying this weight alone.

Sarah sits cross-legged on her neatly made bed, her journal open in her lap and her Bible resting beside her. The room is quiet except for the faint hum of the night outside her window. A soft glow from the lamp on her nightstand casts a warm light over her, highlighting her thoughtful expression as she carefully writes in her journal.

Her pen glides across the page, capturing reflections and prayers. But as she finishes a sentence, her hand stills. A gentle but unmistakable tug pulls at her heart, a feeling she can't ignore. She looks up, her gaze fixed on the far corner of the room as if trying to understand the sudden weight pressing on her spirit.

Setting her pen down, Sarah closes the journal and places it on the bed beside her Bible. She folds her hands together, bowing her head as a calm but determined resolve washes over her. Her voice, barely above a whisper, carries an intimate sincerity.

"Father," she begins, her tone tender yet firm, "I pray for Jasmine. Wherever she is, whatever is happening in her life right now... I know You love her more than anyone ever could."

Her words flow steadily, her faith anchoring her as she speaks. Images of Jasmine flash through her mind—moments of shared laughter, the times she sensed Jasmine was struggling but wouldn't admit it, and the times she seemed so far away despite being right beside her.

"Please guide her back to You," Sarah continues, her voice thick with emotion. "Soften her heart, Lord, and help her see the truth of Your love. Surround her with people who will lift her up, not tear her down. Protect her from anything or anyone that's pulling her away from Your path."

She pauses, her hands tightening slightly as she gathers her thoughts. A deep compassion wells up within her, an unshakable desire to see Jasmine find peace and purpose again.

"Lord, I know You're working," Sarah says softly, her tone full of quiet strength. "Even when we don't see it, even when it feels like nothing is changing—you're always moving. Thank You for being faithful, for loving Jasmine and never giving up on her."

Her voice lowers, her words slowing as she concludes her prayer. "I trust You with her, Father. I trust that Your timing is perfect, and Your plans for her are good. In Jesus' name, Amen."

She lifts her head, opening her eyes as a profound sense of peace settles over her. She lets out a slow, deep breath, her heart feeling lighter even as her concern for Jasmine remains. It's not the heavy, anxious worry it was moments ago, but a hopeful expectation—an assurance that the prayer has been heard and that change is possible.

Sarah closes her Bible with care, placing it atop her journal. She leans back against the headboard, her gaze drifting toward the window. The faint light of the moon filters through the curtains, illuminating the room with a soft, ethereal glow.

"Jasmine," she murmurs quietly, her voice filled with hope, "wherever you are, I pray you feel His love. You're not alone."

She sits there for a while longer, her heart lifted in silent reflection. Though she doesn't know what Jasmine is facing or how long it will take for her to find her way, Sarah feels certain of one thing: the seed of prayer has been planted, and God is at work.

The room was dim, illuminated only by the soft glow of the bedside lamp. She sat on the bed, her face blotchy and streaked with the remnants of her tears. Her phone vibrated again on the nightstand, the persistent buzzing breaking the silence. The name on the screen flashed once more, a name that twisted her heart every time she saw it.

"Not now... not tonight," she murmured, her voice barely audible as her thumb hovered over the "Decline" button. The weight of everything unsaid bore down on her as she let the call ring out.

Moments later, a new notification appeared. The words on the screen made her chest tighten.

"I'm outside. Let's talk. Please."

Her eyes darted toward the window. Outside, parked under the streetlight, was his car. Its sleek form and headlights cutting through the darkness felt invasive, like an unwelcome spotlight on her turmoil. She closed her eyes for a moment, exhaling shakily, before glancing at her reflection in the mirror.

The woman staring back looked fragile, tired, not like herself. She grabbed a tissue, wiping her face in vain, and turned to her closet. Her fingers brushed over the clothes, indecisive. Finally, she pulled out a simple cardigan and a clean pair of jeans, wanting to appear composed despite the storm raging within.

"If he wants to talk, he's going to see the real me," she muttered, her voice steadier now. Pulling her hair back into a loose ponytail, she gave herself one last look in the mirror. Her resolve solidified.

Clutching her phone tightly, she made her way to the front door. Each step felt heavier than the last, as though her body resisted every decision her mind had made. Standing at the door, she rested her hand on the handle, taking a deep, calming breath.

The creak of the front door opening echoed through the quiet house, drawing her attention. She put down the folded laundry and moved into the hallway, her brow furrowed with concern. Her heart sank as she caught sight of her daughter, dressed and heading purposefully toward the door.

"Where are you going?" she called out, her voice firm but laced with worry.

Her daughter's hand gripped the doorknob. She paused for a fraction of a second but didn't turn around. Her silence was louder than any response could have been.

She opened the door, stepping out into the cool night air. The determination in her stride made it clear she wasn't going to stop, wasn't going to explain.

"Jasmine!" The urgency in her voice heightened as she hurried closer, her concern spilling into panic.

But her daughter didn't look back. Her steps quickened as she headed straight toward the car waiting at the curb, its headlights casting long, stretching shadows across the street.

The door swung shut behind her, leaving an uneasy stillness in its wake. She stood frozen in the hallway, her hands gripping the back of the chair for support, her mind racing. Her gaze lingered on the door as though willing it to open again, as though hoping her daughter might change her mind and come back inside.

A faint prayer escaped her lips, a desperate whisper into the stillness. "Lord, keep her safe. Please bring her back."

Outside, her daughter's figure grew smaller in the distance, illuminated only by the stark glow of the car's headlights as she approached. The night seemed to swallow her up, leaving a profound silence in its wake.

The soft rumble of the idling car engine filled the still night air as she approached, her steps measured but hesitant. The car door opened, and he stepped out, his expression carefully arranged—a mix of concern and that practiced charm she knew too well.

"Hey, Jazz," he said softly, his voice low, almost soothing. "Can we talk?"

Her gaze lingered on him for a moment, uncertainty flickering across her face. The rawness of her emotions was still fresh, but something—perhaps curiosity, perhaps the hope for closure—nudged her forward. She gave a small nod and slid into the car without a word.

He gently closed the door behind her, pausing for a brief second as though to gather himself. Returning to the driver's seat, he settled in, his fingers gripping the wheel with a casual ease. The car rolled forward, the soft hum of tires against asphalt blending with the distant sounds of the city as they disappeared into the night.

Inside the house, she stood motionless by the door, her eyes fixed on the retreating taillights. A heavy sigh escaped her lips, her shoulders slumping under the weight of unspoken fears.

"Oh, Jasmine..." she whispered, the words barely audible, her heart torn between love and helplessness.

She slowly closed the door, the latch clicking softly into place. The quiet of the house enveloped her as she lingered in the entryway, her thoughts spinning in circles. The muffled sound of the closing door echoed faintly, leaving her standing alone in the silence, her worry a heavy presence in the empty room.

The room radiated warmth, the soft glow of amber light reflecting off half-filled wine glasses and casting gentle shadows on the walls. Jasmine leaned back into the plush couch, her laughter mingling with Trey's as they exchanged teasing remarks. The earlier storm between them seemed like a distant memory, replaced by a fragile calm.

Trey, ever the charmer, leaned in and pressed a light, lingering kiss to her cheek. His grin was infectious, his confidence unwavering.

"See?" he said, his voice playful yet self-assured. "I told you this night would be great."

Jasmine chuckled, her eyes sparkling with a rare moment of ease. "You were right," she admitted, lifting her glass to his. "I needed this."

Their glasses clinked with a soft chime, the sound punctuating their shared moment of reprieve. Trey tilted his head back, savoring a sip of the wine, while Jasmine allowed herself to relax further into the cushions.

The sudden trill of Jasmine's phone shattered the quiet intimacy, drawing both their gazes to the glowing device on the table. She sighed, her contentment slipping slightly as she reached for it.

"Ugh, who's calling now?" she muttered, the irritation already creeping into her tone.

Her eyes flicked to the screen, where Sarah's name pulsed insistently. Jasmine's expression shifted, her lips pressing into a thin line of annoyance. "Seriously?" she mumbled under her breath before swiping her thumb across the screen to decline the call.

She set the phone down on the table with a bit more force than necessary, flipping it face down as though to block out the interruption entirely. Trey raised an eyebrow, his curiosity piqued but tempered by his amusement at her reaction.

"Everything okay?" he asked casually, leaning back and watching her with a small smirk.

"Yeah," she replied quickly, brushing off his concern. "Just... someone I'd rather not deal with right now."

The phone remained silent, a discarded presence on the table, as Jasmine turned back to Trey with renewed focus. His eyes met hers, and the moment between them seemed to reset, the earlier interruption fading into the background.

Trey's hand found hers, his thumb tracing slow circles on her skin as they resumed their conversation, their voices dipping lower, their laughter softer. The wine flowed, the barriers between them lowered, and the world beyond the cozy glow of the room seemed to blur into insignificance.

Chapter 22

The living room was filled with an air of tension, the soft hum of the ceiling fan doing little to dispel the unease. Mrs. Thompson sat on the edge of the couch, wringing her hands as her eyes darted anxiously between Marcus and Sarah. Her face was lined with worry, the weight of her daughter's recent behavior heavy on her shoulders.

"I don't know what to do," she said with a sigh, her voice trembling. "Jasmine's been acting so distant lately, like she's slipping away, and I can't reach her."

Marcus, seated beside her, leaned forward, his elbows resting on his knees. His expression was calm but concerned, a steady resolve in his eyes. "We've all noticed, Mrs. Thompson. I've been praying for her every day, asking God to guide her back."

Sarah, perched on a nearby armchair, nodded solemnly. Her usually warm and cheerful demeanor was tinged with sadness. "Me too," she added quietly. "It's hard to see her like this. I've been trying to reach out, but... she keeps pushing everyone away."

Her voice broke slightly on the last words, and she quickly glanced down at her hands, clasped tightly in her lap. Before anyone could respond, the sound of the front door slamming shut echoed through the house.

Jasmine stormed into the room, her frustration palpable. Her disheveled hair framed a face flushed with exhaustion and irritation. Her eyes immediately locked on Marcus, narrowing with barely concealed anger.

"What's he doing here?" she demanded, her voice sharp.

Sarah straightened, her expression shifting to one of quiet firmness. "We're just talking about you, Jasmine," she said evenly.

Jasmine's eyes flashed as she turned her attention to her mother. "Shut the fuck up. I asked… Mom, what is he doing here? What are they doing here?"

Mrs. Thompson's lips parted in shock, her composure shaken by the venom in her daughter's tone. "Jasmine, please—" she began, but Jasmine cut her off with a dismissive wave of her hand.

"What is wrong with you, Jasmine?" Sarah interjected, her voice rising as she met Jasmine's glare. "Why are you so blinded by the things of the world? Can't you see what's happening to you?"

Jasmine let out a harsh laugh, shaking her head in disbelief. "Oh, really? And what's going on with you? Since when did you become so obsessed with religious nonsense?"

The room grew heavy with the tension between them. Sarah's face flushed with emotion, her voice trembling as she replied, "I'm just trying to help. Unlike you, who's so wrapped up in your own world, you can't see anything else."

"I don't need your help!" Jasmine snapped, her voice rising. "Or your preaching! Maybe you should focus on your own life instead of trying to fix mine."

Sarah stood, her hands clenched at her sides, her eyes glistening with unshed tears. "Maybe if you weren't so blind, you'd see what's really going on!"

Jasmine took a step closer, her voice dripping with venom. "Advice yourself first, bitch."

The room seemed to freeze, the air crackling with the weight of her words. Mrs. Thompson stood abruptly, her voice trembling but firm. "Jasmine, that's enough! Calm down. We're only trying to support you. But if you can't see that, maybe all we can do is keep praying for you."

Jasmine's expression hardened, her jaw clenched. "Praying?" she repeated bitterly. "That's all you ever do—pray and lecture!"

With that, she spun on her heel and stormed out of the room, the door slamming shut behind her with a resounding thud. The sound echoed through the house, leaving a heavy silence in its wake.

Mrs. Thompson sank back onto the couch, her shoulders slumping. She pressed her fingertips to her temples, her voice a mere whisper. "We just have to keep praying for her. It's all we can do right now."

Marcus leaned back, his face etched with a mixture of sadness and determination. "I agree. We need to stay hopeful, no matter how hard it gets. She'll come around."

Sarah, still standing, wiped at her eyes and took a shaky breath. "I'll keep praying. And I'll keep trying, no matter how much she pushes back. She's my friend, and I'm not giving up on her."

The three exchanged looks, their shared pain and hope knitting them together. Though the evening had been fraught with conflict, they were united in their resolve to stand by Jasmine, even as she stumbled through the darkness of her struggles.

The dimly lit room was a prison of tension and violence, the air heavy with the acrid scent of cigarette smoke and the echoes of Jasmine's cries. She was slammed against the cold wall, her body crumpling slightly from the force. Pain radiated through her ribs, and her wide, tear-filled eyes darted to Trey as he paced in front of her, his movements sharp, his face an unsettling mask of fury.

"You think you can just show up and act like you own everything?" Trey snarled, his voice venomous.

Before she could respond, he lunged toward her, delivering a brutal punch to her stomach. Jasmine doubled over, gasping for air, her hands instinctively clutching at her abdomen.

"Please, Trey! Stop!" she screamed, her voice cracking under the weight of her fear. "I'm sorry!"

Her desperate cries only seemed to fuel his rage. His hand lashed out again, this time striking her across the face with a force that sent her sprawling to the floor. The sharp pain burned through her cheek as she lay there, clutching her trembling body, sobs wracking her frame.

"Please," she whimpered, her voice barely audible. "Just stop! I'll do anything—just stop hurting me!"

Trey paused, looming over her with a cold detachment that was more chilling than his fury. He tilted his head, his gaze filled with contempt as he stepped back, crossing his arms. For a fleeting moment, the room was eerily quiet, save for Jasmine's muffled sobs.

"You brought this on yourself," he said, his tone flat, devoid of emotion. "You need to learn your place."

Jasmine's eyes flickered up at him, her expression a mixture of despair and disbelief. Trey turned, heading toward the table where a pack of cigarettes sat. He took one out, lit it with steady hands, and inhaled deeply. The orange glow of the cigarette tip illuminated his face for a moment, casting shadows that seemed to deepen his menace.

Jasmine pressed her hand to her face, her sobs muffled against her palm. "Please," she choked out, her voice breaking. "I can't take this anymore."

Trey didn't even glance her way. Instead, he exhaled a plume of smoke, the gray wisps curling lazily into the air. He strode toward the window, gazing out with an unnerving calm, as though he were utterly detached from the horror he had just inflicted.

"You think I care about your tears?" he said without turning. "Get yourself together, Jasmine. This isn't a game."

His words cut through her like a blade. She curled into herself, cradling her aching body, the taste of copper lingering in her mouth. Trey, seemingly finished, crushed his cigarette into an ashtray, the sound of the smoldering ember extinguishing echoing ominously in the silence.

Without another word, he walked away, his footsteps heavy and deliberate. The door clicked shut behind him, leaving Jasmine alone in the suffocating silence of the room. Her sobs, raw and broken, filled the space as she struggled to catch her breath. The faint remnants of cigarette smoke hung in the air, mingling with the oppressive weight of her pain and fear. She huddled on the cold floor, trembling, the tears streaming down her face the only solace in an otherwise cruel and unrelenting night.

The room was dimly lit, the only light coming from a small lamp that cast a soft, golden glow. Mrs. Thompson knelt beside her bed, her hands clasped tightly in prayer, her face etched with both hope and concern.

"Lord, please look after Jasmine," she whispered, her voice filled with a quiet desperation. "Protect her from harm and guide her heart. Let her see the light of Your love and find her way back to You. Give her the strength to leave the darkness behind. Amen."

She took a deep breath as she finished her prayer, her body exhaling a mixture of relief and lingering worry. Rising to her feet, she looked toward the window, her heart heavy but hopeful, praying that Jasmine would find the peace she so desperately needed.

Meanwhile, across town, Marcus sat alone in his apartment. The soft rustle of pages filled the space as he opened his Bible, his fingers tracing the worn edges of the pages. With a sigh, he closed his eyes and bowed his head, seeking solace in the stillness.

"Father, I feel a strong urge to pray for Jasmine," he murmured, his voice filled with a deep sincerity. "I know she's struggling, and she needs Your guidance. Please touch her heart and bring her the peace she's seeking. Surround her with Your love and protection. Amen."

He opened his eyes slowly, a sense of determination and concern lingering in his gaze. He closed the Bible, gently placing his hand over his heart. The room was quiet once more, but his thoughts remained focused on the prayer for Jasmine, hoping and trusting that somehow, she would feel the comfort of their prayers, no matter how lost she seemed.

Sarah sat cross-legged on her bed, the Bible resting gently in her lap. Her eyes closed, her hands poised on the book, she began to pray with deep sincerity.

"God, I lift Jasmine up to You. I know she's lost and hurting, and I ask that You find her and heal her. Please give her the strength to overcome her struggles and the wisdom to make the right choices. Let her see Your love and grace. Amen."

She opened her eyes, her face reflecting a sense of hope and resolve. Hugging the Bible to her chest, she silently promised herself to continue praying for Jasmine, trusting that her prayers would eventually reach her.

Later, in Mrs. Thompson's living room, the atmosphere was filled with unity and shared purpose. Mrs. Thompson, Marcus, and Sarah sat in a circle, holding hands as they joined together in prayer. Each of them was determined to stand in the gap for Jasmine, despite the pain they felt seeing her lost.

"Lord, we come together as a family to ask for Your intervention in Jasmine's life," Mrs. Thompson began, her voice steady but full of emotion. "We trust in Your plan and Your love. Please help her find her way back to You, and give us the strength to support her in this journey."

Marcus, his tone full of sincerity, added, "We trust that You will work in Jasmine's life, Father. Please bring her healing and clarity, and let her feel Your presence guiding her."

Sarah, her heart heavy with concern, prayed last, her voice soft but resolute, "God, we believe in Your power and Your grace. We pray that Jasmine will open her heart to You and find peace and redemption."

As they finished their prayer, a quiet sense of uplifted hope settled over them. Each person, though burdened by the weight of their worries for Jasmine, felt a renewed strength in their collective faith. Despite the challenges they faced, they knew they were not alone, and their prayers were their unwavering support.

Jasmine walked into the office, her footsteps confident but her heart racing. As she stepped further in, her eyes caught an unexpected sight—Trey was sitting behind his desk, a woman draped across it in a skimpy outfit, laughing flirtatiously. The woman's giggle echoed in the room, and her clothes barely covered her, sending a wave of disbelief through Jasmine.

She froze, her stomach twisting with a mixture of shock and hurt. She quickly forced herself to steady her breath, trying to suppress the emotions flooding in.

"Sorry, I didn't realize you were busy," Jasmine said, her voice strained but controlled. She turned to leave, her heart pounding in her chest. She could feel her hands trembling as she reached for the door, unable to make herself look back.

Closing the door softly behind her, she stood in the hallway for a moment, trying to regain her composure. The weight of what she had just witnessed settled heavily on her, and she knew there was no going back.

Jasmine hesitated for a moment, then stepped back into the office, her eyes scanning the room. The woman in the skimpy outfit was gone, and Trey was now alone, leaning back casually in his chair. A smug smirk played on his lips as he watched her.

"Alright, Jasmine," Trey began, his tone cool and condescending. "Now that we're alone, I've got a deal for you."

He reached into his desk drawer and pulled out a sheet of paper, placing it on the desk in front of her. Alongside it, he slid a thick bundle of cash.

"Here's an address. I need you to go there tonight by 8 pm. The cash is for your trouble," Trey said with an almost careless air, as if the request were nothing out of the ordinary.

Jasmine's eyes flickered between the paper and the money. A mixture of confusion, frustration, and curiosity flashed across her face as she took it all in. Her gaze narrowed, studying him for a moment before she gave a simple nod.

"Got it. I'll be there," she said, her voice steady but betraying a hint of apprehension.

Trey's smirk deepened, clearly satisfied with her response. "Perfect. I'll be looking forward to hearing about it," he said, his voice laced with expectation.

Jasmine didn't respond. Instead, she tucked the paper and the money into her bag, her mind racing with questions she wasn't ready to ask. Her resolve hardened as she turned and exited the office, her footsteps purposeful as she walked out into the night.

Chapter 23

Jasmine's heart raced as the man's grip tightened around her arm, dragging her further into the dimly lit motel room. Panic surged through her veins, but she forced herself to breathe, trying to think clearly.

"Where do you think you're going?" the man growled, his voice thick with frustration and malice.

Jasmine's mind spun, every instinct screaming at her to escape, but her body was frozen in fear. She twisted her arm in a desperate attempt to break free, but his grip was ironclad. Her thoughts raced as she glanced toward the door, still a few feet away, but it might as well have been miles.

"Let me go!" she cried out, her voice breaking, but the man only laughed, a low, mocking chuckle.

"You think you can just walk away after this? You're not going anywhere," he sneered.

Tears of anger and helplessness welled in her eyes, but Jasmine refused to let him see her weakness. With a burst of adrenaline, she stamped her foot down on his, the sharp pain causing him to loosen his grip just enough for her to wrench her arm free. She stumbled back, her heart pounding in her chest.

She moved quickly, throwing herself toward the door. Before she could reach the handle, the man lunged, grabbing her by the hair and pulling her back with a sharp yank. Her head snapped back, and she cried out in pain, her body crashing into the floor as she struggled to push herself upright.

"You're not going anywhere!" he hissed, his eyes wild with rage.

Jasmine scrambled, her breath shallow, her body aching as she tried to crawl toward the door. Every movement felt like an eternity, but she had to get out. She had no choice.

With every ounce of strength, she grabbed the handle, yanking it with all her might. The door creaked open, and as the man lunged toward her once again, she managed to slip through the crack, slamming it shut behind her.

She didn't look back.

Jasmine's legs trembled as she sprinted down the hall, her breath coming in gasps. She didn't stop until she was outside, the cool night air biting her skin. She didn't care where she was, just as long as she was away from him.

Shaking, Jasmine fumbled for her phone, her hands too shaky to dial Trey's number. The reality of what had just occurred hit her in waves, each more suffocating than the last. She was shaking not just from fear, but from the realization of what Trey had put her through.

Tears streamed down her face as she whispered to herself, "I can't believe this... I can't take this anymore."

And for the first time in a long while, Jasmine felt the weight of her choices, and she knew she couldn't go back to this life. Not ever again.

Jasmine's phone slips from her hand, landing with a dull thud on the pavement. She kneels to pick it up, her hands shaking as she fumbles for it. She stares at the screen, her thumb hovering over the call button again, but she can't bring herself to dial anymore. The silence on the other end of the line echoes louder than any words ever could.

Her body trembles with exhaustion and the weight of everything she's been through. The adrenaline that had once propelled her forward begins to dissipate, leaving her feeling hollow, drained. Her throat feels tight, and she forces herself to swallow, fighting the sobs that threaten to break free.

"I can't do this anymore," she whispers again, barely audible over the sound of her shaky breaths.

Her broken shoe is forgotten in the distance as she starts walking, her steps slow and unsteady. The once-familiar streets feel unfamiliar now, as if the world around her has shifted. Her thoughts swirl, each one more painful than the last.

As she limps forward, her gaze drifts toward the church in the distance, its steeple a beacon of something she can't quite grasp. Maybe it's the comfort of something solid, something unbroken.

Or maybe it's just the need for anything that isn't the nightmare she's just escaped.

Jasmine pushes herself harder, determined to get there, to be somewhere safe, anywhere but here. She doesn't know what she'll find when she reaches the church—she doesn't know if anyone will be there—but she knows she can't keep running from herself, from what she's done, or from the man she's allowed to control her.

The cold night air clings to her skin, and with every labored step, her anger rises. The fury that's been building inside of her since Trey sent her on that mission, since she stepped into that room, is now a roaring inferno, refusing to be ignored.

She reaches the church doors and pauses, her hand resting against the wooden surface. It's a silent prayer of sorts, a plea for something—anything—that might make the pain and shame go away.

With a deep breath, she pushes the door open. The familiar smell of incense and candles fills the air, but there's no comfort in it. The church is empty, save for a few flickering candles and a lone figure in the front pew, deep in prayer. Jasmine hesitates in the doorway, unsure of what to do.

The figure doesn't notice her at first, but Jasmine takes a few hesitant steps into the space, her gaze fixed on the person. It's Sarah, the one person she had hoped would answer the phone, and now here she is, sitting in silence.

"Sarah…" Jasmine's voice cracks as she steps closer.

Sarah turns around, her eyes widening in surprise at the sight of Jasmine. But her gaze softens when she sees the brokenness in her friend's face, the tear-streaked cheeks, the pain and shame that radiates off of her.

Without a word, Sarah stands and moves toward her, arms open wide. Jasmine steps into her embrace, the weight of her sorrow collapsing around her.

"I'm so sorry, Jasmine," Sarah whispers, her voice thick with emotion. "I didn't know... I didn't know."

Jasmine nods, her sobs muffled in Sarah's shoulder as she lets herself finally break down.

Jasmine's eyes catch the sight of her mother's phone, sitting innocently atop the pew, the screen lighting up with another missed call. The sound of Mrs. Thompson's voice, singing in harmony with the choir, drifts through the church. The melody is beautiful, filled with grace, but to Jasmine, it feels distant, like the world she used to know—a world she no longer belongs to.

Her heart aches with each passing ring of the phone, the unanswered calls, the silence that only deepens her isolation. She's never felt this disconnected from her mother, the one person who was always supposed to be there for her.

The choir's voices fill the church with their reverence, but Jasmine can't escape the chaos inside her. She shifts uncomfortably, her gaze never leaving the phone. Part of her wants to reach out, to call again, to try and fix things, but another part of her knows it won't change anything. Her mother isn't going to be there to save her. Not now. Not after everything.

Jasmine takes a shaky breath and looks away from the phone. Her mind races, swirling with guilt and fear. She can't bring herself to talk to her mother like this, not after everything that's happened. The shame, the humiliation—it's all too much.

For a moment, she wonders if she'll ever be able to go back to who she was before. Before Trey. Before the motel. Before the brokenness that now defines her.

But as the choir's hymn reaches a crescendo, Jasmine stands frozen in the middle of the church, torn between the safety of the past and the harsh reality of the present. Her phone buzzes once more, and she glances at it again. Another missed call from her mother.

She takes a step back, away from the pew and the phone, away from the memories of comfort and familiarity. There's no going back. No way to undo what's been done.

With a heavy heart, Jasmine walks toward the exit, leaving behind the church, the sound of the choir, and the world that once felt like home.

Jasmine's footsteps echo in the quiet night as she limps toward the church, the distance between her and the sanctuary stretching endlessly. Each step feels heavier, like the world is pushing down on her, trying to keep her from reaching the only place where she might find solace.

Her heart races, the pain in her body a dull throb as the emotional weight bears down harder with every passing moment. She stumbles once, catching herself against the cold, hard pavement, but there's no stopping her now. She has to get there. She has to make it to her mother.

Tears blur her vision as she wipes her face again, frustration mingling with the sharp sting of fear. Why won't anyone pick up? The question haunts her, echoing in her mind, louder than any prayer. Her mother, Sarah... they should be there for her. They should've been there.

But all she hears is the deafening silence.

As she nears the church steps, Jasmine feels a flicker of hope. She's almost there. Maybe her mother will be waiting for her, maybe there will be comfort—some kind of reprieve from the chaos of her life. She tries to push the fear aside, focusing only on the promise of sanctuary that the church represents.

When she reaches the entrance, the doors are still ajar, casting a soft light onto the steps. The warmth of the light contrasts sharply with the coldness she feels inside. She's on the edge now, teetering between the pull of the familiar and the abyss of her own despair.

Her mother's voice, the sound of the choir in the distance, it's all she can think about as she steps inside. The pews are empty now, save for her mother's phone sitting alone on the nearby seat. Mrs. Thompson's hymn still echoes faintly in her mind, though her presence is absent from the space Jasmine needs her most.

With a deep, shaky breath, Jasmine slowly steps deeper into the church, eyes searching, but finding nothing but the silence.

Jasmine's footsteps echo in the quiet night as she limps toward the church, the distance between her and the sanctuary stretching endlessly. Each step feels heavier, like the world is pushing down on her, trying to keep her from reaching the only place where she might find solace.

Her heart races, the pain in her body a dull throb as the emotional weight bears down harder with every passing moment. She stumbles once, catching herself against the cold, hard pavement, but there's no stopping her now. She has to get there. She has to make it to her mother.

Tears blur her vision as she wipes her face again, frustration mingling with the sharp sting of fear. Why won't anyone pick up? The question haunts her, echoing in her mind, louder than any prayer. Her mother, Sarah... they should be there for her. They should've been there.

But all she hears is the deafening silence.

As she nears the church steps, Jasmine feels a flicker of hope. She's almost there. Maybe her mother will be waiting for her, maybe there will be comfort—some kind of reprieve from the chaos of her life. She tries to push the fear aside, focusing only on the promise of sanctuary that the church represents.

When she reaches the entrance, the doors are still ajar, casting a soft light onto the steps. The warmth of the light contrasts sharply with the coldness she feels inside. She's on the edge now, teetering between the pull of the familiar and the abyss of her own despair.

Her mother's voice, the sound of the choir in the distance, it's all she can think about as she steps inside. The pews are empty now, save for her mother's phone sitting alone on the nearby seat. Mrs. Thompson's hymn still echoes faintly in her mind, though her presence is absent from the space Jasmine needs her most.

With a deep, shaky breath, Jasmine slowly steps deeper into the church, eyes searching, but finding nothing but the silence.

Jasmine walks aimlessly down the street, her steps slow and heavy, as though the weight of the world is pressing down on her. Her heart feels like it's in her throat, a mix of pain and disbelief swirling in her chest. The image of Marcus with Sarah—laughing, smiling, as if everything was fine—replays over and over in her mind, each loop digging deeper into the wound she can't seem to heal.

Why didn't I see it sooner? The question echoes in her head, but she has no answers. She thought there was something between her and Marcus, something real, something that could help her escape the mess of her life. But now she feels like a fool, standing there, watching as everything she thought she knew crumbles in front of her.

Her hands tremble as she pulls her phone from her pocket again, but this time, she doesn't dial anyone. Instead, she scrolls through her contacts, her finger hovering over names—Sarah, Marcus, her mom—but none of them seem like the people who can fix this. She doesn't know where to turn, who to reach out to. The world feels impossibly small, but at the same time, so painfully large, as if she's drowning in it.

Where do I go from here? she thinks again, a bitter laugh escaping her lips, though it's empty. She doesn't know the answer. Not yet.

She stops at the corner, staring out at the neon lights of the city, feeling the emptiness of it all settle over her. The noise of the street—cars honking, people talking—feels distant, muffled, as if she's encased in some kind of shell.

She takes a deep breath, trying to steady herself, but the air is thin, the weight of everything pressing harder.

Jasmine looks down at her phone again, her thumb brushing over the screen absently. A part of her wants to call Sarah, but then she stops herself. What's the point? she thinks. Sarah has her own life now, a life that doesn't involve her. And Marcus... well, Marcus had already moved on without her.

Her gaze falls to the sidewalk, and she starts walking again, each step taking her farther away from the diner, from Marcus, from everything she thought was stable. She needs to go somewhere, anywhere, just to escape the sharp pain that's gnawing at her.

Her mind spins, not knowing where her feet are taking her, but she just keeps walking.

Jasmine's voice trembles as she speaks to the night, her words broken and filled with so much pain. The world around her feels like a blur, the sounds of the street, the honking of cars, and the distant chatter fading into the background. All that remains is her, walking through the dark, stumbling toward something she doesn't know but desperately needs.

Her steps are slow, like each movement takes everything out of her. The weight of the church steeple in the distance draws her in, its towering presence offering a strange sense of comfort. But the closer she gets, the more she feels like she's walking into an abyss, unsure if anything will change once she steps inside.

God, can You hear me? Her mind screams, her thoughts scattered like shards of glass. Can You even hear someone like me? The question hangs in the air, unanswered.

She makes it to the church doors, her breath ragged, her chest tight. Her hand reaches for the door, but it feels heavier than she anticipated. Her fingers linger on the cold metal, trembling.

I've messed up so bad... I don't know how to fix this... Her thoughts are jumbled, but the one thing that feels certain is her need for something—anything—outside of her pain.

With one final, shaky breath, Jasmine pushes the door open. The soft glow of the church's interior beckons her, but even as she steps inside, she feels like an outsider in a place meant for solace.

Her footsteps echo in the silence of the empty church, the distant sound of the choir still faintly lingering in her memory.

Jasmine walks toward the altar, her eyes blurry with tears, her body heavy with exhaustion.

Please... help me, God. Her prayer is a whisper, barely audible against the weight of everything she's been carrying.

She sinks to her knees at the front of the church, her hands clasped tightly in front of her, eyes squeezed shut as if praying for some kind of miracle. The soft glow of the candles around her flicker, casting warm shadows against the stone walls.

Jasmine bows her head, feeling the emptiness deep within her heart, and waits. She doesn't know what for—maybe just a sign that she's not alone, maybe just a sense of peace.

But for now, in the quiet of the church, she allows herself to cry.

Chapter 24

The streetlights cast a dim glow on the rundown motel as she steps out of the cab, clutching the paper with the address. Her heels click on the pavement as she walks briskly toward the entrance, her expression a mix of anticipation and anxiety.

Inside the motel lobby, she approaches the tired-looking receptionist, asking for room 13. After receiving directions, she heads down the corridor, her steps quickening with every passing moment.

At the motel room, she knocks on the door, and it creaks open, revealing a man in his 40s. His smile is too warm, his eyes lingering on her with a predatory gleam. She shifts uncomfortably.

He enthusiastically welcomes her inside. As soon as she steps in, his demeanor changes, and his inappropriate touch makes her pull back in alarm.

"What are you doing?" she asks, shocked.

His smile fades, frustration flashing across his face. He curses under his breath and dials a number, pacing angrily.

"Who did you send me? She's not even worth fifty bucks!" he snaps into the phone.

Her heart sinks as the reality of the situation dawns on her. She quickly begins gathering her things, but before she can make it to the door, the man slams it shut and grabs her arm, pulling her back toward him.

"Where do you think you're going?" he growls.

Her breath quickens as she struggles in his grip, trying to break free, but his hold tightens.

Eventually, she stumbles outside, battered and broken, her clothes torn and her hair a mess. One of her heels is snapped, forcing her to limp down the street. Her phone clutched in one hand, tears streak down her face. But beneath the devastation is a deep, simmering anger.

"I can't... I can't do this anymore," she whispers to herself, scrolling through her phone in a trembling hand, hoping for someone—anyone—to pick up. She presses a contact, hoping for a familiar voice on the other end.

The phone rings... and rings... then goes to voicemail. Her hope slips away, replaced by frustration.

"Thanks, thanks a lot," she mutters bitterly, feeling abandoned by the ones she trusted. Her eyes well up again, but she fights back the tears, dialing another number.

As she limps down the street, her phone rings again—her mother's name flashing on the screen. She wipes her tears away with her sleeve, desperate for some comfort, but when the call goes unanswered, her frustration builds.

She continues to walk, each step heavier than the last, her heart growing colder with every unanswered call. As she nears the church, a flicker of hope rises within her. Her mother must be inside.

She takes one more step, then another, her heart and legs faltering as the weight of the night presses down on her. Her phone vibrates in her hand, but she doesn't look at it. She only looks at the church doors, which are softly illuminated from within.

When she reaches the entrance, the doors are ajar, light spilling onto the steps. The familiar melody of a choir reaches her ears, but as she steps inside, the warmth of the church only contrasts with the cold emptiness she feels inside.

The pews are empty now, and the soft sound of hymns lingers faintly in the distance, but her mother is nowhere to be seen. Her phone sits on a pew, abandoned, a silent reminder of unanswered prayers.

With trembling hands, she reaches for the door handle, opening the door to the warmth inside. She steps into the sanctuary, her breath shaky, tears continuing to fall. She knows now, more than ever, that she's completely lost, but somehow, standing in this sacred space, there's still a flicker of hope within her.

Taking a deep breath, she kneels at the altar, head bowed, eyes closed, hands clasped tightly together. She whispers softly to herself, asking for forgiveness, unsure of how to make things right, but hoping that somehow, by being here, she might begin to heal.

Jasmine doesn't hear her mother's footsteps at first—she's too lost in her own sorrow, her head bowed, the weight of her emotions pressing her deeper into the floor. Her hands tremble as she clasps them together, the silent prayer escaping her lips between sobs.

But then, the sound of soft footsteps reaches her ears. She looks up, her eyes still blurred with tears. Through her blurred vision, she sees her mother at the front of the church, her figure framed by the dim light streaming through the stained-glass windows.

Mrs. Thompson moves quickly toward her, her expression filled with concern, understanding, and an overwhelming love that makes Jasmine's heart ache even more. The choir behind her stands in quiet support, their eyes gentle and knowing.

"Jasmine," her mother whispers, her voice breaking as she kneels beside her, enveloping her daughter in her arms.

Jasmine falls into her mother's embrace, her sobs deep and raw, as if the dam holding her grief back had finally broken. She clings to her mother, her body shaking with the weight of everything she has been carrying. It's the first time in so long that she feels truly seen, truly held.

"I'm so sorry, Mom... I've been... I've been lost," Jasmine whispers between sobs. "I don't know how I got here. I didn't know what to do... I was so alone."

Mrs. Thompson holds her tighter, her hands running through Jasmine's hair, soothing her like she used to when Jasmine was a child, when the world hadn't been so heavy.

"You're not alone," her mother whispers softly, her voice a gentle reassurance. "You'll never be alone. I'm here. God is here. We'll find our way together."

Jasmine's heart calms, even if just a little, the comforting warmth of her mother's presence beginning to heal the wounds that have been festering for so long. She leans into her mother, allowing herself to finally breathe, to finally rest.

"I'm so sorry, Mom... I've made so many mistakes... but I'm ready now. I want to change. I want to be better."

Her mother pulls back slightly to look at her, her hands cupping Jasmine's face, her eyes filled with both love and sadness. "You don't have to be perfect, Jasmine," she says gently. "You just have to be you. And you are enough."

Jasmine nods, the tears still flowing, but now they feel different—like a release, a cleansing. She feels the presence of something greater than herself in the quiet of the church, in the warmth of her mother's embrace.

Together, they sit there in silence, the echoes of the choir's final hymn wrapping around them, bringing peace where there was once only turmoil.

She steps inside, the familiar scent of the church hitting her, grounding her even in her broken state. Her heels click lightly on the tiled floor as she slowly walks down the aisle, her head hanging low, her arms wrapped around herself as if trying to hold everything together.

Her steps slow as she nears the front of the sanctuary. The choir's voices swell in the background, their music soothing the storm inside her. Her voice cracks as she continues, barely above a whisper.

"I need You. I can't do this without You... I don't want to live like this anymore."

She kneels down, her knees hitting the cold tile, and clasps her hands together.

"Please... take me back. Show me the way... I'm ready to follow You, whatever it takes."

Her body shakes with silent sobs as she lowers her head, unable to hold back the flood of emotions any longer. Suddenly, she hears footsteps approaching. The voices of the choir grow louder as they finish their song, and then... silence.

She lifts her head, and a figure appears at the front of the church. A familiar figure, having heard the door, hurries toward her, their heart swelling with relief and gratitude.

The figure kneels beside her, wrapping her in a warm, comforting embrace. Others begin to gather around, offering silent support, their presence speaking volumes.

A gentle hand rests on her shoulder, and a voice, soft and reassuring, speaks.

"The Lord's mercy is new every morning. You're not alone in this. We're here for you, and so is He."

Another voice follows, just as kind and welcoming.

"God's arms are always open. It's never too late to come home."

Overwhelmed by the warmth of their words, the comfort surrounding her, she clings to the one holding her close. Her voice is barely audible, but she speaks with deep gratitude.

"I don't deserve this... thank you all."

The one holding her tighter brushes her hair from her face, speaking softly, her voice filled with deep love.

"God never left you. And neither did I. We're going to walk this road together, one step at a time."

She nods, feeling the flicker of hope stir inside her. Her heart still heavy, but now with the possibility of healing, she allows herself to believe that maybe, just maybe, this moment is the beginning of something new.

The door slams open with a deafening crash, and police officers rush in, their boots pounding the floor, their flashlights slicing through the darkened office.

"Clear the room! Sweep everything!" one officer yells, his voice sharp and commanding.

The team moves quickly, tearing through the space with practiced precision, opening drawers, flipping through papers, and tossing aside objects with urgency.

One officer mutters under his breath, "This guy's been living the high life..." He pulls open a drawer, revealing stacks of cash, neatly piled on top of each other like trophies.

Nearby, another officer sweeps a pile of paperwork aside, his eyes widening at the sight of a small mountain of drugs. Plastic bags, scales, and syringes are scattered across the desk like they've been carelessly left behind.

"Looks like we hit the jackpot," another officer says with a smirk, surveying the chaos.

The lead officer steps forward, his gaze hardening as he takes in the scene. His voice is cold, devoid of any emotion.

"Bag it all up. He's done."

The officers snap photos, carefully collecting evidence, their movements swift and methodical as the reality of Trey's operation crumbles in a single, devastating raid. The once-glamorous facade of his criminal empire now lies shattered on the floor, the weight of it all crashing down on him in this one moment.

Trey lounges on the plush couch, his feet kicked up on the coffee table, lost in the glow of his phone screen as he scrolls through messages, a carefree smile spreading across his face. He's basking in the luxury of his life, oblivious to the impending storm.

Suddenly, the front door slams open with a deafening crack.

"Trey Williams! Police! Get down!"

The shout rips through the calm, and Trey's smile vanishes in an instant. His heart leaps into his throat, and before he can even process the words, panic floods his face. He jumps to his feet, eyes wide.

"What the—?"

Before he can react, two officers are on him, their movements swift and calculated. They slam him to the floor, and before he can make a move, they pin him down, the cold bite of handcuffs snapping around his wrists.

"You can't do this! I didn't do anything!" Trey struggles, his voice desperate, but the officers are relentless. His fight is futile against their strength.

One officer, towering over him, leans down with cold finality. His voice is firm, devoid of sympathy.

"We found your stash. Drugs, cash — enough to bury you, Trey. It's over."

Trey's eyes widen, the weight of the words crashing over him. His mind races, his breath short, as he tries to grasp at any last shred of hope.

"This is a mistake! You don't understand!" His voice cracks, pleading, but the officers aren't listening. They pull him to his feet, the handcuffs digging painfully into his wrists.

Trey's world is unraveling. The escape he's been searching for, the illusion of control he once had, is gone.

He's helpless as they drag him toward the door.

The red and blue lights of the police cruisers flash, casting an eerie glow over Trey's face. His expression is a mix of fear, disbelief, and shock. The once pristine street outside his grand house is now filled with police vehicles, their presence a stark contrast to the life he once led.

Neighbors peek out from their windows, their faces filled with curiosity, as they witness the fall of the untouchable man. He's not the powerful figure they once admired; now, he's just another criminal.

Rough hands push him into the back of a police car. The door slams shut behind him with a finality that echoes in his mind.

As the cruiser pulls away, Trey's gaze is fixed on the world outside, his life unraveling in front of him. The extravagant parties, the power, the control—everything he once reveled in—has evaporated, leaving only an overwhelming void.

Inside the backseat of the police car, Trey sits, his face pale, a reflection of his own brokenness staring back at him in the window. The city lights flicker past, casting fleeting shadows on his expression. His eyes are wide, hollow, consumed by the realization of what's to come. His world, once vibrant and full of promises, is now a distant memory.

The police radio crackles, its static blending into the quiet. But for Trey, it's drowned out by the deafening sound of his future slipping away, piece by piece.

Jasmine sits in her room, her Bible open in front of her. She reads with a deep focus, her heart absorbed in the words. A sense of calm has settled over her, and she reflects quietly, marking passages that speak to her. Her journey has led her here, and she's determined to understand it fully.

On a Sunday morning, she walks into the church, her attire modest and her expression thoughtful. She takes a seat, her attention fixed on the pastor as he speaks of redemption and forgiveness. His words resonate within her, sparking a quiet, hopeful conviction in her heart.

Later that evening, Jasmine kneels beside her bed, her hands clasped in earnest prayer. Her eyes are closed tightly as she pours out her heart, her voice a quiet whisper of repentance and sincere hope. She asks for guidance, her commitment to change unwavering.

Midweek finds her at a Bible study group at church, where she participates actively in the discussions. Her insights are thoughtful, and her engagement shows a deepened understanding of her faith. With every conversation, Jasmine's resolve grows stronger, and her spiritual journey becomes more meaningful.

Back at home, she sits at the kitchen table, reading her Bible once more. The room is quiet, save for the soft rustle of pages. Mrs. Thompson enters, and without saying a word, sits beside her, placing a comforting hand on Jasmine's shoulder.

"I'm so proud of you, Jasmine. I've seen you grow and change," Mrs. Thompson says, her voice warm with love.

Jasmine looks up, a gentle smile curving her lips. "Thank you, Mom. I feel like I'm finally on the right path."

The next Sunday, Jasmine stands before the congregation, dressed in white, ready for her baptism. The ceremony symbolizes her commitment to her new faith, a public declaration of the transformation she has embraced.

In the park one day, Jasmine walks with a Bible in hand, greeting people she passes with a serene smile. Her calm demeanor reflects the peace she's found within herself, a peace that now radiates outward to everyone she meets.

Later that evening, Jasmine sits at her desk, writing a letter with determination. She looks down at the words she has written, a quiet confidence in her eyes as she finishes the letter.

To herself, she whispers softly, "This is the beginning of something new. I'm ready for what's to come."

Other Books By The Author

Tangled Hearts

Silent Vision

Silent Vision 2 Code Name Echo

Man Up

Woman Up

Couple Up

Marriage is it worth the fight

Sheltered Hearts

WYGDN what you gonna do now

Empowering the Future

Artificial Love

Beyond Loss

Silent Vision 3 Ghost Hunter

NEXT (Negative Evaluation and Xchange Trade)

Ungrateful

The MInd